CUSTOMERS
HATE

WHAT
CUSTOMERS
HATE

DRIVE FAST AND SCALABLE GROWTH BY
ELIMINATING THE THINGS THAT DRIVE AWAY BUSINESS

NICHOLAS J. WEBB

HARPERCOLLINS
LEADERSHIP

AN IMPRINT OF HARPERCOLLINS

Published by HarperCollins Leadership, an imprint of HarperCollins Focus LLC.

Any internet addresses, phone numbers, or company or product information printed in this book are offered as a resource and are not intended in any way to be or to imply an endorsement by HarperCollins Leadership, nor does HarperCollins Leadership vouch for the existence, content, or services of these sites, phone numbers, companies, or products beyond the life of this book.

ISBN 978-1-4002-3668-8 (eBook)
ISBN 978-1-4002-3667-1 (TP)

Library of Congress Control Number: 2021952501

Printed in the United States of America
22 23 24 25 26 LSC 10 9 8 7 6 5 4 3 2 1

*I would like to dedicate this book
to my amazing family:*

*My wife, Michelle;
our daughters, Taylor, Madison, and Paige;
and my son, Chase.*

CONTENTS

CONTENTS

ACKNOWLEDGMENTS

I would like to acknowledge my learned colleagues in the customer experience ecosystem for all that they have taught me.

I would like to particularly thank Dr. Ray Power, Matti Palo, MD, and my team at Learnlogic and Leaderlogic.

PREFACE

For over four decades, I've been using my expertise to help organizations improve their customer experience (CX). During much of this time, my work within the CX ecosystem was characterized by a dutiful adherence to the conventional wisdom of customer experience best practice. Like every other professional, I genuinely believed you could use surveys, promoter scores, and other one-size-fits-all approaches to understand what customers loved. Having learned what they wanted, you'd then sell it to them. The process seemed very logical and straightforward. In fact, my bestselling book on customer experience, *What Customers Crave*, was the epitome of that approach.

It's undeniably true that you must give your customers what they crave. That will never change. That's your ultimate goal. If you fail to do that, your business will die.

But after years of working in the trenches, shoulder to shoulder with organizational decision makers, I realized that finding out what customers loved was only half the battle. In today's hypercompetitive and fast-paced marketplace, your customers are very sensitive to what they *hate* about your brand, company, or service. These feelings of hate (that's just the word I use—it's short and simple) can have just as much influence on their buying decisions as what they love.

Whether you're selling to consumers or business-to-business (B2B), perfection in the marketplace does not exist. When making buying decisions, customers are faced with an array of imperfect choices. They look around and say, "The first choice is too expensive. The second choice isn't exactly what I want. The third choice can't be delivered quickly. The fourth choice makes me assemble the product. But I need to buy one of them. So, which choice do I hate the least?"

No company, brand, or service enjoys 100 percent love. There must always be some degree of hate in the mix. Hate is a source of friction, and if there is too much friction, the process of moving products and services—regardless of their high quality—into the hands of consumers will grind to a halt.

In my busy consulting practice, I've learned that uncovering what your customers hate about your brand, company, or service is just as important as what they love. Yet I've seen many well-intended executives spend millions of dollars on training and customer insight programs that have had zero effect on improving their customers' experiences. Too many such organizations are living in the past. In a time of massive and continuous disruption, they're trying to optimize obsolete systems, policies, and training programs. What they really need to do is press the reset button and look at the world with fresh eyes.

While writing this book, I saw that some organizations were reducing the hate of friction, and in doing so were crushing the competition.

If disruption is the problem, and it is for most organizations, then the solution is relentless innovation. Customer experience is an innovation discipline. The best organizations in the world lean into change by developing sophisticated customer experience innovation activities. They are making their journey into understanding their customers from the perspective of learning not only what they love, but what they hate. They're taking their hate insights and turning them into friction-free, relevant, and valuable experiences for their customers, and as a result they've become disruptive leaders. These disruptive leaders reap the rewards. They attract and keep the best talent. They enjoy customer promotion, customer satisfaction, significantly lower marketing costs, and—most importantly—scalable growth and profitability.

This book is the product of many years of frontline work with innovative companies and their customers. I hope you'll find its new approach can make a difference to your company, brand, or service.

INTRODUCTION

Since the dawn of civilization when people first traded trinkets for fur pelts, merchants have tried to figure out what made their customers happy and therefore willing to buy from them. If they somehow learned the secrets of customer satisfaction, sellers then endeavored to deliver the solutions. This process continued for thousands of years, in most cases carried out by simply talking to the customer and asking what they wanted.

In recent times, and especially in the digital era, sellers have tried to uncover this information scientifically, using a complex array of tools including data collection, surveys, promoter scores, focus groups, and more.

Despite the expense and effort, so much of this has been in vain. In both the consumer and B2B markets, hundreds of millions of dollars are spent each year on consumer preference research and marketplace data collection, and yet the results are often incomplete and provide inaccurate customer insights. In fact, the overwhelming majority of today's companies fail to gain the inside knowledge that drives the ultimate goal of happy and loyal customers. They dutifully prioritize their marketing budgets, and yet their social media ratings are not where they should be, and most of their customers either hate them (at worst) or merely tolerate them (at best).

Don't take my word for it—let's try a simple exercise. Set a timer for one minute and then list five companies you absolutely *love.* If you're like most people, chances are you'll struggle to find an example of just *one* great organization that delivers predictable and exceptional customer experiences. There are tens of millions of organizations, yet most of us search to find one example of an organization that delivers an experience that makes us smile.

It can seem like a complicated problem, but if you're like me, you want a simple and easy-to-understand path forward that offers both fast and sustainable results. That's what this book delivers.

In these pages, you'll learn the benefits of shifting from a singular focus of *making your customers happy* to include *eliminating what your customers hate.* This is not a play on words or a riddle. The overwhelming majority of organizations are polishing the brass on the deck of the *Titanic* while their customer experience ship is sinking. The data shows that most organizations deploy on fractional customer experience solutions rather than using a triage approach to first fix their gaping abdominal wounds.

If you want to be the best experiential option for a customer, you need to begin by eliminating the hate.

Why does customer hate matter so much?

Haters hold the secret to your success—or lack thereof. Knowing what your customers love is useful, because they *want* to buy what they love. It's what they *hope* for. But knowing what customers hate is equally useful.

Organizations that have the highest degree of sustainable growth and profitability most often present themselves to the market as the *best possible option.* Again, I'm not suggesting perfect, I'm just suggesting the best option. In order to be the best option, most people have to hate you the least. It's a pretty simple formula, but for some reason most organizations completely miss it. Here are just a few reasons why you should strive to understand what the haters hate:

- When compared to customers who love you, haters are far more likely to share with friends and social media the fact that they hate you. Reviews that have specific hates are a powerful deflector of potential customers.

- Haters provide far more granularity about what they hate. Lovers tend to speak in a general vernacular, whereas haters get really specific. They will say *exactly* what displeased them. As I'll reveal in the pages ahead, this specificity can be very useful to your company.

- Haters are more emotionally energized than lovers, and their language is typically far more impactful.

- Haters have market power. A few bad reviews can knock you out of the competitive arena, costing your organization dearly—in some cases, millions of dollars.

- Haters want to talk to anybody who will listen about what they hated. That includes you, and reaching out to haters is the ultimate form of building customer insights.

And perhaps the most powerful reasons of all:

- Haters are inventors who offer up specific suggestions regarding what companies can do to stop the hate.

- Haters who are converted to lovers are some of the best promoters for an organization or brand.

Starting with eliminating what customers *hate* will help solve the underlying problem while providing far better insights into what customers *love.*

What Customers Hate will show you how to avoid the common pitfalls that have damaged some of the best organizations and best teams in the world, and how to change the philosophical view of customer experience so you can learn that customer experience is actually an innovation activity.

To help you separate the hate from the love your customers feel for you, this book provides a powerful new tool: the Net Customer Experience (NCX). You get it through the RealRatings system, which provides an accurate measurement of what your customers hated and loved across the five touchpoints and a range of hate/love personas.

In the RealRatings survey method, your customers give you lovepoints and hatepoints. Lovepoints are measured across four experiences aiming toward being loved. The four possible answers are "unliked," "liked," "loved," and "really loved."

Hatepoint measurements are measured across four experiences that trend toward hate. They are "not good," "bad," "hated," and "really hated."

By subtracting the hatepoints from the lovepoints to produce a score, NCX represents the net total of what the experience was like for customers. This score is very useful because it's expressly asking what a customer didn't like and what a customer did like at a specific touchpoint. This provides actionable insights that your organization can use to rapidly fix the dislikes to significantly improve your NCX score.

By leveraging the power of RealRatings and the Net Customer Experience, this book will show you how to significantly reduce the cost of customer acquisition. It will reveal how to keep your customers and turn them into promotional machines for your organization. You'll learn how to build a culture of institutional happiness and how to use powerful tools like the customer experience hackathon. You'll have everything you need to know to thrive in a time of major competition, massive disruption, and hyper consumerization.

The book will dive into a thorny subject that many business owners try to avoid: the direct connection between *employee happiness* and *customer happiness*. The real secret—and equally important fact—is that the reverse is true: there's a cause-and-effect link between *employee misery* and *customer hate*. There's no way your customers are going to be happy and feel good about their interactions with your business if your employees are projecting negative energy.

With that in mind, the book provides powerful insights on how to make organizational happiness an enterprise strategy. Customer experience is not a software solution, outdated best practice, promotion score, or survey result. This book demonstrates the need to redefine customer experience not as a marketing campaign or a fractional customer experience gimmick but as an *innovation activity*. To do this right, especially in a hyper-competitive marketplace, you need the superpower of customer experience innovation (CXI).

The process is easy to understand: to produce happy customers, you must not only give them what they want, you must also reduce the irritating things they hate—and be sure to include your own employees in the equation.

Ready? Let's get started!

CHAPTER 1

YOUR CUSTOMERS HATE YOU.
GET USED TO IT!

Imagine you're on a road trip, driving from your home to a scenic destination a few hours away. You and your companion have been enjoying the day, but now the sun is setting and you're both getting hungry for dinner. Because you're in an unfamiliar area, you don't know the local restaurants. To find one, you ask your phone for suggestions of eateries near you.

On the screen you see a selection.

The nearest restaurant is a national fast-food burger franchise.

"Ugh—there's no way we're eating there," you say. "I hate that stuff. I want real food."

The next one is a chain pizza place.

"Nope," says your companion. "Their pizza tastes like cardboard."

"Here's one," you say. "Mom's Home Cooking. Good food and spirits."

Your companion agrees that you should have a look at Mom's Home Cooking. After driving for fifteen minutes, you pull into the gravel driveway of the restaurant.

"Uh-oh," says your companion. "This place is scary. Look at all the motorcycles parked here! I think Mom must be a member of a local biker gang. I don't think this particular establishment is for us."

You get back on the highway. The sun is nearly gone and you're really hungry. You scroll the list. "There's a seafood place a few miles up ahead. Fisherman Joe's."

"It looks okay in the photo," says your companion. "Let's check it out."

You drive another fifteen minutes and pull up in front of Fisherman Joe's. It looks pleasant, so you park the car and go inside.

The moment you step through the door, your companion turns to you and says, "Do you smell that rancid odor? That's a bad sign. They cannot be selling fresh fish. We need to get out of here."

You turn around and get back in the car. By now it's dark and you flip on the headlights. "I'm *starving*," you say. "What's the next choice?"

"Pasta Garden," says your companion. "Four miles ahead."

With your stomach growling, you drive to Pasta Garden. You park and hurry from the car. The menu is posted outside. You read it. "To be honest, I don't want pasta," you say.

"We have no choice," says your companion. "We're going inside. You can have chicken or veal."

You go inside. The place is pleasant enough. "Inoffensive" would be the best term.

"We've got to eat," your companion whispers. "How bad could it be?"

"I'm sure we'll survive," you reply as the hostess ushers you to your booth.

You dutifully order your meals and have a barely drinkable bottle of wine. After dinner, you pay the check and, with your appetite satiated, go back to your car.

"How was your chicken?" asks your companion.

"Like rubber." You shrug. "But it was food. Let's get going."

Let's step back and consider what just happened. That evening, you spent your money at one of five businesses competing for your consumer dollars. Of the five, Pasta Garden was the winner. They got your business. But should the owner of Pasta Garden be celebrating his victory over his four rivals? Should he think that because you chose to patronize his restaurant that you loved the experience and would go there again, and even recommend it to your friends?

Absolutely not. You did not choose Pasta Garden because you loved it and would add it to your list of favorite dining spots. You chose it because of the available alternatives; *you hated it the least.* In fact, you'd be happy to never set foot in the place again as long as you lived. There was plenty about the business that you hated—it was boring, had rubbery food, mediocre wine, and unexceptional service. The only thing you loved about it—if I can use the term loosely—was that the food was edible, it filled your stomach, and it didn't make you sick. At that moment in time, when you were desperate to eat something, your lukewarm love for Pasta Garden outweighed your considerable hate for the place.

On the Net Customer Experience tool, the restaurant's love-points just barely outnumbered its hatepoints. While it's better than the alternative—being totally hated—*this is no way to grow a business!* To grow a company, you need to elicit not merely grudging acceptance from your customers but genuine attraction. Here's why: While the owner of Pasta Garden may think he owns his market and needn't worry about competitors, his blithe ignorance will be shattered when a new restaurant opens down the street that offers its patrons much more to love and much less to hate. Suddenly his patrons will have a real choice, and Pasta Garden will be on the losing end. You've seen this happen over and over again in every industry, from retailing to electronics to automobiles. The complacent business owner who ignores the power of hate may survive from one day to the next, but only as long as he or she faces no competition. When a strong competitor emerges—which it always will—the customers will flee to the newcomer.

Being loved by your customers should be your goal, and every business must be focused on providing value and a superior customer experience. But the recognition of the flip side of the coin—the fact that consumers hate many businesses—should alert you to the very important fact that *reducing what your customers hate is just as important as increasing what they love.*

PERFECTION IS NEVER ATTAINABLE

In response to being handed this book, a typical business owner might say this:

> *This book is called* **What Customers Hate.** *I don't understand. My customers are my customers because they love the products and services I provide. If they truly* **hated** *my company or my products, they would not be my customers. We live in a highly competitive marketplace, and every consumer has many choices. Therefore, anyone who is my customer must also love what we sell. If they do not love what we sell, then they are not my customer. That's why it's impossible to talk about what customers hate—especially* **my** *customers.*

In a perfect Utopia, where every choice is available all the time, this rationale might have some value. For example, if you manufactured the perfect peppermint toothpaste and could sell it in an instant transaction, and your potential customer wanted peppermint toothpaste, then that person would buy your perfect product. If the customer didn't want peppermint toothpaste, they would not buy from you. It would be very simple!

This belief is based upon the *ideal marketplace*, in which every customer can buy exactly what they want, when they want it, and have it instantly delivered into their hands. Another name is *frictionless commerce*, a theoretical trading environment where all costs and restraints associated with transactions do not exist.

In the ideal marketplace, the customer would be able to say, "I need to clean my floors, and my vacuum cleaner is old and broken. I need a new one, and I'm ready to pay five hundred dollars for one with all the latest features." At that moment, the perfect vacuum cleaner would appear in the supplies closet, and five hundred dollars would disappear from the customer's checking account. Poof! It would happen in an instant.

If your company could *not* fulfill this order, then the person would simply buy from some other provider.

That's a nice scenario, but it does not reflect the real world, which is much more complicated. All too many times, such as in the story of Pasta Garden, consumers must settle for the solution they hate the least. While driving in search of a place to eat, we rejected the first four restaurants because there was just too much to hate. At Pasta Garden, there was less to hate, and it won. It pays to know what your customers hate—and remove it from their experience.

No company is perfect. Neither are its customers. We live in a world in which we strive for perfection, but it's never attained. We're always one step behind what we hope to achieve. At Pasta Garden, the owner may be sincerely trying his best to present a quality product, but there are shortcomings. In every transaction, there's always some friction. People make mistakes, machines break down, the weather prevents shipments from arriving on time—there are many reasons why even a well-functioning system can be flawed.

The Number One Law of Customer Experience is this: *Your customers are always settling for second best.* Don't be offended, because "first best" is perfection in the ideal marketplace. No customer can have perfection. Because they can't have perfection, they look around for the next best thing.

Having been denied the ideal solution, in the process of settling for what they can get, the customer will look at a company or product from two distinct perspectives:

1. How much do I *love* this company? As the seller of a product, your goal is to maximize these good feelings. (This is the subject of my bestselling book *What Customers Crave*.)

2. How little do I *hate* this company? As the seller of a product, your goal is to minimize these bad feelings. (The subject of this book.)

These questions, and their answers, have equal weight. As we saw with Pasta Garden, your potential customer will be swayed by the sum of the two. If the scales tip in favor of loving your company, congratulations! You'll have—or keep—your customer, at least in the short term. If the scales tip in favor of hating your company, then sorry, you'll lose the sale and the customer.

Company leaders who accept the reality described earlier are one step ahead of the deniers—but they're not yet out of the woods.

The problem is that leaders are tempted to look at the problem of customer hate very narrowly. They think, "Okay, we live in an imperfect world, in which customers must choose between flawed options. Obviously, if our product is superior, customers will love it, and will choose us. Our products will speak for themselves, and sell themselves."

To support this view, they'll point to the fact that customer word of mouth is the most powerful marketing tool, and if the product is outstanding, then customers will tell each other, and everything will be ducky.

This naïve viewpoint completely overlooks the *customer experience* in its totality.

HOW DO I HATE THEE? LET ME COUNT THE WAYS . . .

Let's dive deeper into the many ways your customers can rack up hatepoints against your company.

Your Product or Service

As we've agreed, we live in an imperfect world. This imperfection extends to your product or service.

Okay, I'll concede that if you're in the business of selling sand and gravel, a commodity that hasn't changed in ten thousand years, you might be able to claim that your product cannot be improved and is therefore perfect. But you're the exception that proves the rule.

Products and services are designed to solve a problem or somehow change the living conditions of the consumer. Products cannot be perfect for two reasons:

1. **We live in a flawed world.** The materials and processes that we use to create products are limited in their capabilities. Mistakes in manufacturing happen. Design flaws

exist. They can happen at the very highest levels, such as in the Boeing 737 MAX passenger airliner, grounded worldwide between March 2019 and December 2020 after 346 people died in two crashes—Lion Air Flight 610 and Ethiopian Airlines Flight 302. The problems included poor design of the anti-stalling system and a lack of pilot training. The twenty-month grounding cost Boeing an estimated $20 billion in fines, compensation, and legal fees, and indirect losses in the form of 1,200 cancelled orders valued at more than $60 billion. It also gave Boeing a bad reputation, which it had to work mightily to restore.

Product defects can happen on an everyday level, too, such as the 2009 salmonella outbreak in peanut products that killed nine people and sickened hundreds. The source was traced back to the Peanut Corp. of America, an obscure, privately held peanut processor in Georgia that supplied hundreds of food brands. As news of the recall spread, wary consumers shunned *all* peanut butter by *every* brand, driving down industrywide sales by 25 percent. Peanut Corp. declared bankruptcy and went out of business. The Georgia Peanut Commission estimated at the time that, as a result of the disaster, America's peanut producers lost $1 billion between sales and lost production.

2. **Products become obsolete.** In this book, I'm going to talk a lot about innovation and how its pace is accelerating. The product you launch with great fanfare this year may be old news next year. Your customers will hate the product of yours they currently own when they see that your competitor has introduced one that's better.

Obsolescence is also a factor in the price curve of new technology. Take, for example, electric cars. The price driver of electric vehicles has always been the batteries. Otherwise, EVs are astonishingly simple vehicles with far fewer moving parts than gas cars.

Prices of EVs are determined by the cost per kilowatt-hour of the energy produced by their batteries. This price is continuing to trend down, and according to a report from energy research firm BloombergNEF (New Energy Finance), by 2023 the market average should be $101 per kilowatt-hour. This will approach the price point where experts expect the cost of EVs to match the prices of comparable gas-powered vehicles. If federal and state tax credits are still available at that time, it's likely they could make an EV cheaper than a gas car to buy.

Since Tesla introduced its lithium-ion battery-powered Tesla Roadster in 2008, the price of electric batteries has been dropping. In 2020, the average global price for batteries hit a new low of $137 per kWh, representing a whopping 89 percent drop from 2010, when the price was $1,100 per kilowatt-hour.[1]

This means that many price-conscious consumers will hold back from buying EVs until the price is no more painful than a gas car. And consumers who bought an electric car in 2020 may be dismayed to see the same car selling for much less just a few years later.

Fortunately, on the love-hate scale, in 2020, buyers of EVs tended to be enthusiastic "early adopters" who loved the new technology and knew they were paying a premium to experience it.

• • •

Your Customer Experience

Every sales transaction involves a process, which I'll discuss in greater depth in the pages ahead. Sometimes the process is very brief, almost perfunctory, while other times it can be prolonged, even over a period of months in B2B settings or in the consumer world for a major purchase such as a house or commercial property. Regardless of its length or complexity, customers always want to feel good about the process of selecting, buying, and using the product, and they want it to go smoothly.

The customer experience can be mapped out along a series of five "touchpoints," which I'll discuss in greater depth in the pages ahead. Suffice to say that at every touchpoint, you have the opportunity to amaze and delight your customer and make them fall in love with you. You also have an equal opportunity to turn them off, discourage them, and even make them hate you. Every touchpoint can become either a lovepoint or a hatepoint.

The choice is yours.

Some people will say, "You're being overdramatic. Customers aren't that sensitive to every little thing. They want a product, so they go to the store and buy it. Or they click on the website. They go through the process, and they get what they want. No drama."

In response, I would say, "What's your profit margin? Three percent? Five percent? How much of that narrow margin can you afford to lose to a competitor who's working just a little bit harder than you to create a positive customer experience at every level?"

Take the case of the world's biggest and most ubiquitous retailer, Walmart. With over eleven thousand stores worldwide and revenues of over $559 billion, you might think that the chain could afford to relax and coast on autopilot. But according to Macrotrends.com, as of January 2021, Walmart's net profit margin was a razor-thin 2.42 percent. In 2018, it dipped as low as 1.01

percent. To put that into perspective, a New York University report on US margins revealed the average net profit margin was 7.71 percent across different industries. As a rule of thumb, 5 percent is a low margin, 10 percent is a healthy margin, and 20 percent is a high margin.[2]

In this century, Walmart has learned to face, and rebuff, a fierce competitor—Amazon.com. In response to the growing size of the number two retailer, Walmart ramped up its online presence at Walmart.com. In a move appearing to be a response to a similar price-lowering strategy Amazon initiated in August 2019, it subsidized the price cuts it demanded of some third-party sellers offering their goods at Walmart.com. While third-party vendors provide many of the goods sold via Walmart.com, much of the online inventory is Walmart's own. The company offsets thinner margins with more volume.

A key feature of Walmart's profitability is its low-cost production. With over eleven thousand locations, it's able to negotiate rock-bottom prices from suppliers. It's also able to distribute fixed costs over a much broader base, allowing Walmart to offer lower prices than most of its competition.

Walmart's continued success lies with its relentless adherence to the one simple goal that Sam Walton formulated in 1962 when he opened his first store: "Help people save money so they can live better." The goal is to help people live better lives as a result of the money they save by shopping at Walmart. With the money they keep in their purse or pocket, they can buy other stuff, or maybe go on that family trip to Disney World. It's a nuanced distinction, but an important one.

Is there something to hate about the Walmart in-store shopping experience? Of course! There are many people who loathe Walmart stores and find that patronizing a Walmart store makes them feel like a lab rat navigating a gigantic maze. But millions of other people aren't bothered by the low-rent, industrial vibe of the big Walmart stores. They see the bare-bones presentation as proof that they're saving money, and going there as a sort of social event, where they see other people and can chat with the friendly Walmart greeters. This is the secret that Sam Walton knew: even if your store is just a big, ugly metal box, you can make up for it with customer service. As he said, "There is only one boss: the customer. And he can fire everybody in the company from the chairman on down, simply by spending his money somewhere else."

Your Company's Reputation

Customers want to enjoy the shopping experience, however brief it may be. They want to feel as though they've made the best choice. They also want to feel good about *where* they're spending their money. When you're looking to build up lovepoints and minimize hatepoints, this component of the transaction is becoming increasingly important.

Customers like to identify with the brands they use. They know that every time they spend a dollar with a company, that dollar will be used to support the company and the full range of its activities. In today's socially aware culture, many consumers are keenly interested in the "backstory" of the company whose products they buy. They ask, "What are the company's labor policies? Where is their manufacturing done? Is the company socially responsible? Are the products made or harvested in a way that's sustainable?"

For example, consider the outdoor gear company Patagonia. As a socially responsible company, they've put into place a wide range of forward-thinking initiatives. They build robust environmental and animal welfare responsibility programs to guide how they make their materials and products, they've pledged 1 percent of sales to the preservation and restoration of the natural environment, and much more. Their products are also very high quality. As a result, Patagonia's customers love them a lot and hate them very little.

As we'll explore in the pages ahead, it can be difficult to determine what makes customers either love you or hate you. Sometimes, the issues you think will trigger a negative reaction from customers are instead met with just a shrug.

Take retail giant Amazon. As a purveyor of consumer goods, the company is trying its best to achieve the ideal, frictionless marketplace. To order a product, you go to their website, choose your item from the roughly 350 million available, and make a few clicks. In a regional Amazon fulfillment center, robots and human employees jump into action to "pick" your item, pack it, label it, and ship it. In many cases, you can have it in your hands the very same day.

Sounds good, doesn't it? Here's where it gets tricky. While Amazon has millions of customers who love the service it provides, it has many critics, particularly regarding how it has treated employees. In 2019, writer Emily Guendelsberger took a job at an Amazon fulfillment center (that is, warehouse) in Indiana. Echoing the reports of many Amazon workers, she wrote, "It took my body two weeks to adjust to the agony of walking 15 miles a day and doing hundreds of squats. But as the physical stress got more manageable, the mental stress of being held to the productivity standards of a robot became an even bigger problem." Indeed, the relentless drive for efficiency included the scan gun she used to do her job. The device doubled as her personal digital manager, precisely monitoring and timing every task. When she completed one task, the scan gun not only immediately gave her a new one but also started counting down the seconds she had remaining to do it. This and other intrusions by the scanner created "a constant buzz of low-grade panic," and the sheer boredom of the work left her feeling, in her words, "as if I were losing my mind. Imagine experiencing that month after month."[3]

Despite the negativity many consumers feel about Amazon as a company, the retailer keeps growing. For the fourth quarter ending December 31, 2020—the height of the COVID-19 pandemic—Amazon reported net sales of $125.56 billion, a 43.6 percent increase from $87.44 billion in the same quarter in 2019. It had added 175,000 employees in the fourth quarter and increased its fulfillment warehouse footprint by 50 percent compared to the same period in 2019.[4]

This acceptance of Amazon among people who are looking to buy something is the result of a relentlessly seamless shopping experience. Amazon remembers you and what you've bought in the past, makes it incredibly easy to find the product you want, and whisks you through the checkout process with just a few clicks. Because the customer experience has been scrubbed of anything the customer might hate, most people will say to themselves, "I need a certain product. Should I get in the car and drive to the store to buy it—and hope it's in stock—or spend one minute of my time, make a few clicks on Amazon, and have it delivered to my home tomorrow?"

It's fair to say that few people love Amazon. After all, there really isn't anything to love about it. The shopping experience is dry and matter-of-fact. People shop on Amazon because *there's nothing to hate about it. Amazon wins by being the least objectionable of the available choices.*

——————————TAKE ACTION!——————

The most important action you can take right now is to repeat this mantra out loud: "Our customers judge our company, brand, or service not only on what they love about it but what they hate about it. We pledge to recognize this reality, and henceforth strive to both increase what they love and identify and decrease what they hate. This is the future of our organization."

CHAPTER 2

TOUCHPOINT #1:
THE PRE-TOUCHES

We live in a world composed of two groups of people: those who are selling products and services, and those who are customers. When they interact, we have commerce. The more commerce we have, the better the world.

Commerce doesn't just happen by magic. To a certain extent, such as the buying of water and sewer services from a municipality, commerce can happen without outside stimulus. But the vast majority of transactions are voluntary, and require an effort, and interaction, on the part of both seller and buyer.

At some point in time in his or her life, your customer has no knowledge of your company or your products. This state of unawareness may last only a short while after birth, or well into adulthood. And of course if your company is newly formed, then most of your prospective customers will have no knowledge of your product. If in 1996 you would have asked consumers if they had heard of an online bookstore named "Amazon," the vast majority would have replied, "Huh? No."

Over time, consumers find companies and their products, and purchases are made. Sometimes customers buy the product just once, and never again, and sometimes they like the product so much they'll buy it over and over again.

Thus is created the customer life cycle or journey. The customer's journey with your brand is characterized by a series of steps, with five stations or touchpoints. (Some analysts assign dozens of touchpoints. That seems a bit excessive.) At these touchpoints, the customer and the company have one or more interactions. These interactions may be brief or prolonged. Each one is important. At every touchpoint, the company has the opportunity to create either a feeling of love by the customer for the brand or a feeling of hate.

The sum total of the customer experience over the five touchpoints—which may extend in time to cover many years—is the Net Customer Experience (NCX). This is the measurement of what the customer hated and loved across the five touchpoints, given a range of hate/love personas.

Hatepoints are measured across four negative experiences: not good, bad, hated, really hated.

Lovepoints are measured across four positive experiences: unliked, liked, loved, really loved.

NCX represents the net total of what the experience was like for customers by subtracting the hatepoints from the lovepoints to produce a score. This score is very useful because it's expressly asking what a customer didn't like and what a customer did like at a specific touchpoint. This provides actionable insights that an organization can use to rapidly fix the dislikes to significantly improve their NCX score.

In this chapter and the following four, I'll reveal and discuss the five touchpoints, and the risks and opportunities of each as they relate to the overall NCX score.

Touchpoint #1 is the pre-touch stage.

In this stage, the prospect (not yet a customer) develops an awareness of your brand. While it can happen non-digitally, these days it's more likely to happen on a connected device, through the internet. It can happen at any moment in the prospect's life. It can happen in childhood, when you climb into your mom's Toyota minivan, or watch a Disney movie, or have a Domino's Pizza delivered. Brand awareness can be formed at a very early age, and consumer products companies like it that way. The sooner in life you become loyal to a brand, the better. Disney is very good at this. The company wants every child in America to know the song "Let It Go" from the movie *Frozen*, and as every parent wearing earplugs can attest, they've damn well succeeded.

As we get older, we start buying things for ourselves. We find new products and brands through advertising, word of mouth, and by doing our own research.

Even today, pre-touches can be analog. If you have an actual physical location, what does it look like to potential customers driving by? How about when they park their car, walk up, and open the door? Are they greeted with smiles or indifference? Remember the story of the five restaurants. Four of the five flunked the pre-touch test. Only Pasta Garden won, because it was the least terrible choice.

The digital pre-touch is where your potential customers check you out online. They google you, and look for reviews on Yelp, Amazon, or other sites. They'll visit your website to look around and get acquainted. They're educating themselves about your online reputation before they actually engage with you.

There are likely to be many pre-touches over a period of time. For example, in the world of advertising, it's long been said that seven exposures to an advertisement are required for the consumer to pay attention to the ad and its message. This is an approximation. Some ads, like the famous Apple television commercial titled "1984," which aired during the Super Bowl that same year, become massively consequential with just one viewing. Other ads, most notably ads for commodities like cheap beer and auto insurance, must be aired constantly to keep the brand in the mind of the consumer.

The pre-touch stage is where the customer experience begins. Put more simply, it's where the prospect determines if they could love you. Remember, they are looking for a high degree of relevancy, value, and clarity wrapped up in a friction-free experience. Underestimating the value of this touchpoint is asking for failure. Its importance will only grow over the years.

THE SALES FUNNEL

Marketers like to compare the sales process to a funnel or pipeline. I used this same imagery when discussing innovation in my book *The Innovation Mandate*. Basically, the opening of the sales funnel is very large. It serves as an entry point for anyone who could possibly be a customer. The space before they enter the funnel is the pre-touch. They're out there in the marketplace, developing an awareness of your product or brand, but there has been no interaction with the sales process. Making these definitions can get tricky because it's entirely possible—in fact likely—that the prospective customer will have an interaction with your product *without being a customer*. For example:

- Your friend pulls out her phone and shows it to you. "It's nice," you say. "What brand is it?" Your friend tells you it's the newest Samsung. "I like it," you reply. You have just had a pre-touch moment with the product, and this time, you feel no hate, only love. Score one lovepoint for Samsung!

- Your friend's house is damaged in a storm. The next day you go to see her. You ask her how she's doing. She says, "The roof needs to be repaired, and I'm trying to contact my insurance company. They told me the adjuster can't get here until next week! What am I supposed to do, put out garbage cans to catch the leaks? I have ABC Insurance Company, and boy, do I hate them!"

- It's your birthday, and your mom gives you a new pair of jeans. "Don't worry about the size—you can easily exchange them," says your mom. Sure enough, the jeans are too small. You call XYZ Retailer to find out how to exchange them. The customer service rep says you need the receipt, you need to go to the mall twenty miles away, you need to do this and that, and if they don't have your size you can get store credit . . . blah, blah, blah. So now, even though you're not a customer and never wanted to be a customer, you are caught up in their machine. You've been forced into the first-touch stage of the sales funnel, which I'll discuss in the next chapter. With your heart filled with hate, you drop off the jeans at the nearest Goodwill store. Score one big hatepoint for XYZ Retailer.

As you can see, plenty can happen to your brand image in the big world beyond the entrance to your sales funnel!

Once the individual chooses to enter the wide opening of the funnel, they are considered a prospect. I'll discuss your interactions with them at the next touchpoint.

Here are a few more of the things that can go wrong during the pre-touch moments before the individual enters the sales funnel.

THE PROSPECT HEARS SOMETHING BAD ABOUT THE BRAND

This is extremely common, and in the age of social media it's more significant. The prospect can see critical comments on Twitter or Facebook, read or see on TV a negative news item, or be told by a friend about their negative experience with a product or company.

As more and more companies establish and use their own social media accounts, on which they post information and other marketing materials and attempt to interact with consumers, the possibilities for mistakes grow.

Here's a painfully hilarious example.

On Valentine's Day in 2020, the Massachusetts Bay Transit Authority (MBTA)—also known as Boston's bus and subway system—launched a contest asking Twitter audiences to tweet a sixty-second video about something they *loved* about the MBTA. Those who entered the contest could win a round-trip JetBlue flight for two.

Keep in mind that this is Boston's ancient and overpriced public transit system, about which satirical songs have been written. ("Charlie on the MTA," which tells the absurd tale of a man named Charlie trapped on Boston's subway system, was a big hit for the Kingston Trio in 1959.) In Boston, *everyone* hates the MBTA. The contest was greeted by howls of delighted derision as MBTA riders invented all sorts of ironic reasons why they "loved" the MBTA, from being chased by rats in the stations to locked restrooms and trains that derailed whenever it snowed.

The MBTA used to have an advantage not shared by most companies: it's a public monopoly. No matter what horror stories they heard, people who rode the subway to work had no other choice. If they hated the subway, that was no sweat off the MBTA's back. The MBTA could rack up endless hatepoints and just shrug them off. But then Uber and Lyft came along and disrupted the market, giving subway riders an affordable choice. A 2019 report from researchers at the University of Kentucky found the introduction of transportation network companies (TNCs) including Uber and Lyft are having an impact on subway and bus ridership. Their results suggested that for each year after a TNC entered a market, heavy rail ridership could be expected to decrease by 1.3 percent and bus ridership by 1.7 percent. As *Business Insider* reported, ride-hailing effects are so substantial that, if the trend continued, bus service in cities studied could decline nearly 13 percent over a period of eight years.[1]

HATE BEGETS MORE HATE

In our digital era, the pre-touch stage is primarily the process of researching a product, service, or brand through a connected device. When a potential customer searches your business, products, or services, they will find ratings on social media sites. Consumer ratings are incredibly impactful, as they represent a community of customers talking specifically about your organization.

In researching this phenomenon, I found that if your company goes from a five-star to a three-star review on Yelp, you can lose up to 70 percent of your revenue. This means that customers follow the crowd, and—rightly or wrongly—they hate companies that other people hate. If your organization isn't addressing your bad reviews, that oversight could cost you your business.

This reaffirms my belief that it's fundamentally important to *find out what customers hate and then eliminate that experiential element immediately.*

Unhappy customers are far more likely to post a negative rating than are happy customers to post a positive rating. In simple terms, this means your haters have much more power over public opinion, simply because they are more vocal.

Just as important as customer ratings are the ratings posted by your own employees on sites such as Glassdoor. Not only do these ratings spill over into the realm of your customers, but they're read by potential employees. As I'll discuss in the pages ahead, the success of your company is directly linked to the engagement, productivity, and positive attitude of your employees.

As reported by Recruiterbox, Software Advice found in a survey that 48 percent of responding job seekers had used Glassdoor at some point in their job search. One-third of job seekers said a company needed at least a three-star rating before they would apply. An Indeed survey found that 83 percent of job seekers are likely to base their decision on where to apply on company reviews, and 46 percent will weigh a company's reputation heavily before accepting a job offer. And a Bayt.com survey found that 76 percent of professionals research a company online before considering a job opportunity.[2]

If you have employees who hate your company, then your troubles are just beginning, my friend!

SEARCH FRICTION

If you're looking to lead your market and customer experience, you need to be readily accessible to your customers. That means you have to be extremely thoughtful about search engine marketing, search engine optimization, and omni-channel marketing. Customers need to find you quickly and easily, and they hate it when they can't. This may not seem like a customer experience issue, but it is. Not finding you or your company is friction, and customers dislike friction. If you're having this problem, then add another hatepoint to your total.

LANDING PAGE RELEVANCY

Your digital strategy has to be hardwired into your customer experience strategy to make certain that your pre-touch moments are exquisite and hate-free.

In developing your beautiful and clear pathway for your customer's journey, you need to structure your website as a series of highly relevant landing pages. I do a lot of work in healthcare, including for providers of orthopedic surgery. This practice area includes areas of surgical intervention such as knee replacement, hip replacement, and shoulder replacement. If someone is looking for knee replacement surgery and they land on the homepage of an orthopedic surgery practice and they can't quickly find the specialty they want, which is knee replacement surgery, they'll become irritated and leave.

Score another hatepoint.

In your advertising, you should always feature keywords specific to a need or problem. If a customer searches "knee replacement surgery," and they go to your Google advertising or other digital advertising, it should take them to the knee replacement page. The page must always match the customer's "search intent." Is this a marketing strategy? Yes, but it's also an important part of how you deliver frictionless interaction, speed, and relevancy in the pre-touch stage. Organize your site so that each individual service or product function has its own micro site that delivers exquisite relevance, and you will eliminate the hate. This also will significantly reduce the "bounce rate"—that is, customers backing out of your site because they're not willing to go on a search expedition to find what they want.

In your integrated customer experience strategy, work with your digital team to make certain that your customer experience strategy aligns with your omni-channel marketing strategy.

This rule also helps weed out the customers who aren't going to love you. Remember Mom's Home Cooking? If in fact the restaurant was a favorite biker hangout, then this should have been featured on the restaurant's website. There should have been photos of the parking lot full of chopped Harleys, and happy bikers inside. Doing this would serve to both reinforce the love felt by their core customer—bikers and other adventurous types— while serving as "truth in advertising" for everyone else. Customers really hate it when the product is not in perfect alignment with what they've seen—and have come to expect—in the marketing message.

NO VALUE DISPENSING

In simple terms, your digital property is nothing more than a value dispenser. Your website should be structured in such a way that it is delivering real and meaningful value to your site visitor. The overwhelming majority of organizations essentially suspend a brochure on the internet that they call a website. I once had a professional service firm as a client, and 80 percent of his website was devoted to talking about how great he was. There was virtually no value to the visitor whatsoever in reading about this professional and how great he was, and it became tedious very quickly.

This is not an uncommon problem. The overwhelming majority of specialty practice websites are nothing more than a personal promotion site for the physician. Customers want to know that you know what you're doing, but they're more interested in you delivering proven value. If you look at websites that deliver the best experiences for their customers, they are dispensing free e-books, white papers, value-based videos, and free offers that are of conspicuous value to their site visitor.

Remember, the customer is totally self-centered, and rightfully so. They want to know one thing: "What's in it for me?" This is the ironclad rule of WIIFM. The customer has a need or a problem. They want information that will tell them that you understand their problem and can provide the solution. Empty braggadocio is no substitute for real value.

I find that many organizations need to press the reset button when it comes to the simplicity and value that their websites provide. Take a look at a great organization such as Lemonade.com, an online insurance company. This company has an insanely simple website that allows you to get an insurance policy in about ninety seconds. It lets you file a claim and get paid in roughly the same time. If you're looking to buy insurance and you visit this website, you know that dealing with them is going to be beautiful just by looking at the website.

So ditch the brochure, build a value dispenser, and start scoring lovepoints!

YOU MAY HATE US—
BUT YOU'LL LOVE OUR MASCOT!

Speaking of insurance companies, consider the plight of the big auto insurers: GEICO, Progressive, Liberty Mutual, Allstate, and Farmers. It will not surprise you to learn that consumers *hate all auto insurance companies*. This is because auto insurance is a product that, except if you live in New Hampshire or Virginia, your state *forces* you to buy. If you never have an accident, you'll just keep paying and paying, with no benefit to yourself.

Here's the surprise: the big auto insurance companies have realized that customers hate them. Rather than despairing over this, they all, without exception, pour millions of dollars into overtly comic TV advertisements. These ads have become little sixty-second sketch comedy pieces that are, in many cases, every bit as good as what you'll see on *Saturday Night Live*. The first to embrace humor was GEICO, in 1999. During a Screen Actors Guild strike that prevented the use of live actors, the company invented the GEICO gecko, who in his singsongy English accent pleaded for people who were confusing "gecko" with "GEICO" to stop phoning him. The GEICO gecko was a big hit, and instead of loathing all the boring auto insurance ads and changing the channel when they came on, viewers got a laugh and watched the ads. Now every insurance company has their comic spokespeople, perhaps none more effective than the Progressive Insurance gang headed by Flo, wearing her white nurse's pantsuit, and her revolving cast of bumbling sidekicks. Stodgy ol' Liberty Mutual Insurance developed the dimwitted duo of a human named Doug and his sidekick, an actual emu named the LiMu Emu. Farmers Insurance stages wacky car accidents hosted by Hollywood actor J.K. Simmons. State Farm gives us "Jake," the hapless call center agent who, clad in his trademark khaki pants and red shirt, talks to customers on the overnight shift.

The strategy is brilliant. The companies are saying to consumers, "Hey, we know you hate buying auto insurance. You probably hate us, too. But the law requires you to buy the product from one of us. We're all the same—auto insurance is basically a commodity. So we're going to try and make it fun. And maybe—just maybe—you'll love us a little bit!"

TAKE ACTION!

In terms of your marketplace reputation, you may think that "no news is good news"—that is, unless a customer complains to you directly, then your reputation in the marketplace must be good. Unfortunately, this is a very naïve point of view that can cost you dearly. Your customers may form an opinion about your company, brand, or service long before you have any direct contact with them. In these pre-touch moments, they may hold tremendous hate derived from some third-party source. You owe it to your brand to constantly monitor what's being said about your company on social media and other means of communication. Also, make sure your employees are happy and therefore won't be a source of negative talk.

CHAPTER 3

TOUCHPOINT #2:
THE FIRST TOUCHES

As your mom always said, "First impressions last a lifetime." So it goes with the first touches. They set the theme for how your customer will forever perceive your product, brand, or service. If you have a bad first touch, it's really hard to fix. Conversely, if your first touch rocks, then you can easily build on that and build up your lovepoints.

Customers checked you out in the pre-touch stage, but there was little or no interaction. They saw your ad on TV, or walked past your storefront and peered in the window. They saw your product at a friend's house, or read a review in a consumer magazine. If they visited your website, they didn't click on anything—they just poked around and left.

At the first-touch stage, for the first time, they actually engage with you. As with all the touchpoints, the key is to build an exceptional experience across all your customer types. Identify those types, understand what they want, then deliver it to them—exceptionally.

The first touchpoint is too often riddled with customer hate-points. It includes:

The car dealership that attacks you with a pushy salesman that makes you recoil and leave.

The medical clinic that makes you fill out thirty-page forms and wait for an hour to see a doctor.

How about the hotel that has one person checking in guests, and there are thirty people in line?

I could literally list hundreds of examples of how a bad first touchpoint can destroy an enterprise. So why do we do it? Executives and leaders are so busy spending money on customer acquisition and looking at new ways to cross market to existing customers that they're clueless as to how bad they are at the first touchpoint.

Eliminating hate significantly increases revenue, drives customer promotion, boosts brand value, and paves the way for scalable growth and profitability.

The first step toward reducing hatepoints is to *know your customer*. While it's true that customer demographic data is expanding exponentially, the most important thing about your customer is *not* their age or ethnicity. No, it's their expectations for their interaction with your company and its systems and people. Human beings make buying decisions based not only on a rational assessment of the market but also on the emotion connection and how they're treated by their peers who own and operate businesses they patronize. While every customer is a unique individual, they fall across a spectrum of customer types.

Let's review some of the customer types and how your approach with them should vary accordingly.

Before we begin, the one super-important fact you must believe is that all the stories and theories about "Baby Boomers" and "Millennials" and "Gen X-ers" having different customer expectations are *total nonsense*. This kind of phony classification by age doesn't work, and if you try to do it, you will make many potential customers hate you, and you will lose business. The human personality is determined at a young age, and as you move through the stages of life, it doesn't change. A twenty-five-year-old college student may have different consumer expectations from her classmate, but the same expectations as her eighty-year-old grandmother.

On the other hand, the best way to fail in the hypercompetitive marketplace is to attempt to deliver a one-size-fits-all customer experience. Every company serves a market segment, and within each market segment there are customer types who want to engage your products and services differently based on their individual hates and loves.

Here's an example. Every morning, I go for a run with a group of guys who live in my neighborhood. We're all men, about the same age, fully employed (aside from disruptions due to the pandemic), and economically affluent. Demographically, we might look the same. But under the surface, we're all very different. One is politically conservative, and another is liberal. One is super-religious, and another is an atheist. Despite being from the same one-dimensional market segment, as customers we have very different expectations—not necessarily about a particular product, but about the process and the touchpoints of how that product is sold to us. If our customer experience was based on our individual loves and hates, then our customer service experiences would be different.

Done correctly, incredible and relevant customer experiences can be delivered that appeal to different types across all five touchpoints.

• • •

THE FOUR CUSTOMER PERSONAS

Here are the four overall customer personas, each with their own set of expectations. They are the Driver, the Analytical, the Amiable, and the Collaborator. Each persona includes adults of all ages, ethnicities, and gender identification. If you're in sales, then you need to quickly identify which persona has approached you (or you are approaching), and instantly "mirror" their personality. This is not meant to be insincere or phony. The goal is to make the customer feel comfortable and meet their expectations of what they want.

If you're designing a website, then you need to ensure that the site's architecture accommodates every type, so that every customer finds exactly what he or she wants.

#1: The Driver

These are goal-oriented decision makers. They enter your store—either brick-and-mortar or online—armed with the knowledge of what they want. If they see what they want, they'll buy it on the spot. They want as frictionless an experience as possible.

- **How to make the Driver hate you:** Chat with them. Waste their time. Be unclear in your information. Try to squeeze them for their last dollar. Try to steer them toward a product you'd love to sell to them but they don't want. Ask them to wait while you "talk to the manager."

  If the Driver is dressed casually, or is a different ethnicity from you, then condescend to them. The high-powered CEO who walks in wearing jeans and a sweatshirt will *really* hate you if you act like a snob.

On your website, make them jump through hoops to buy your product. Add hidden charges at checkout. Then ask them to complete a customer satisfaction survey at the end.

- **How to make the Driver love you:** Smile. Be forthright and confident about what you're offering—don't beat around the bush. Be prompt and courteous, but not "chummy." Stick to the business at hand. Know your product and its benefits. Don't talk too much—let them take the lead in the conversation. This customer is looking for an efficient and knowledgeable facilitator, and you need to make that expectation a reality.

   They may ask questions about product features or benefits. This is mostly to confirm that you know what you're talking about. Keep your answers short and factual.

   Yes, it's true that some Drivers can be insufferable blowhards. (Any luxury car dealer in Hollywood can regale you with horror stories of ego-driven stars.) If your customer wants to be treated like royalty, go ahead, play the part as long as there's no cost to you.

   Beware of fraudsters. If a flashy "Driver" shows up in your store because he wants to impress his gullible girlfriend and has no intention of buying, feel free to press him until he invents an excuse to come back later.

#2: The Analytical

This customer wants detailed information about the product or service. They need facts and figures, and they love to ask questions. They do their homework, and pore over every possibility before making a purchase. Much like Drivers, they don't seek small talk. They like to stay on topic while still discussing each option to ensure they are making the right decision.

They may also want to know about the company itself and how products are sourced. Social responsibility is important to an increasing number of customers, so be prepared.

- **How to make the Analytical hate you:** Provide cursory answers. Appear to be impatient. Don't have a thorough understanding of your product. Be condescending. Try to push them into a sale.

  On your website, bury the relevant product and company information so it's hard to find.

- **How to make the Analytical love you:** Know your product and be on your toes. The analytical is looking for a subject matter expert, so be that person. Provide them with accurate answers to their questions or concerns. Don't take it personally if they try to fact-check you, because it's all part of them reaching their comfort zone. Above all, be patient!

  On your website, be sure that the product and company information is robust and easy to find.

#3: The Amiable

The polar opposite of the Driver, this customer wants you to be their friend. To them, it's very important that you understand them and why they want the product or service. They have a strong need to belong and relate to a group. They don't just do business; they want to include you in their network of friends. Intensely loyal, they have a circle of professionals attached to every need in their life—the same doctor, lawyer, mechanic. Out of fear of having to trust someone new, they rarely stray from the group. They are dependable, "go with the flow," customers that want the best for everyone around them.

On the plus side, if they have a positive experience with you and your product, they'll proclaim it on social media. They make the very best brand ambassadors.

- **How to make an Amiable hate you:** Be brusque. Recoil when they touch you on the arm. Be impatient, and push them toward a sale. Act like your time is short and you can't be bothered with information about their recurring medical condition, the lousy weather, or traffic jams.

  On your website, provide only skimpy information. Don't have any photos of happy customers or five-star reviews.

- **How to make an Amiable love you:** Make the entire shopping experience aesthetically pleasing and relaxed. Treat the Amiable as if they were visiting your own home. Make them feel welcome and special. Often with the Amiable, they want the interaction to be successful (they are optimistic people), so in a sense, the sale is yours to lose. To keep them on track, gently remind them that you are there to help them.

  On your website, provide plenty of customer testimonials and good reviews. Amiables want to know they are in good company.

  Warning: Some extreme Amiables never want to buy anything—they're just lonely people who want someone to talk to. Let them lead the discussion. Eventually, they'll get tired and leave.

#4: The Collaborator

Collaborators need to make decisions that are supported by a consensus. They might bring their friends or family members into your store to help them make a selection. Because Collaborators tend to be tactful and adaptable, they're often pleasant to work with. The downside is that they will rarely make a decision on the first visit and may take repeated touches because they need their group to reach a consensus. This is the person who will say they need to ask their spouse or partner before they commit. In the B2B world, they may delay a purchasing decision so they can run the idea by their teammates.

- **How to make a Collaborator hate you:** Try to pressure them to make a quick decision. Say things like, "Well, this offer won't last forever!" Fail to provide the documentation they ask for. Ignore or be rude to the friend or colleague the Collaborator has brought along for support. In the B2B world, fail to follow up with supporting information. Fail to include other team members who need personal attention.

- **How to make a Collaborator love you:** Be patient. Arm them with a generous amount of documentation they can show to their group. When they leave and come back a few days later, remember them and offer to work with them to answer any questions the group (or spouse) may have.

    Make sure you remain patient, and be sure to facilitate any discussions among the Collaborator's group so everyone's questions and thoughts are addressed. Sometimes the people whom collaborators bring along are uninformed and obstructionist. Be super-patient with them. Like a politician, you may need to do a lot of "grip & grin" sessions!

HARD SELL, NO SELL, SOFT SELL

Everyone knows the story of Goldilocks and the three bears. Goldilocks enters the home of the bears, and being hungry, heads for the kitchen. For some reason, the bears have left their bowls of porridge on the table. Goldilocks samples the first one and rejects it because it's too hot. The next one is too cold. The third one is just right. She loves it.

In the sales funnel, the first-touch stage represents the first interaction your prospect has with the company—or more precisely, the company's sales machine. The marketing effort has done its job to educate and entice the prospect, who now has taken the proactive step of coming into your store or entering your website to actually look for a product or service.

Your sales system must be like the third bowl of porridge: not too hot and not too cold. It needs to be just right.

By too hot, I mean the "hard sell." The hard sell is based on the ridiculous belief held by some "sales experts" that goes like this: If the salesperson uses the correct psychological tools on the prospect, the salesperson will be able to convince the prospect to buy the product. If a sale is not made, then the salesperson has failed. The hard sell consists of a series of enticements and veiled threats that will lead any prospect to the inevitable conclusion that they should hand the salesperson their credit card.

The problem with the hard sell is that when you succeed in coercing someone into buying something they may not really want, then later, when the pressure is off and the customer considers the interaction and the product they were talked into purchasing, they'll realize that they do not really want or like the product. They will return it or even cancel their credit card authorization. Remember, consumer protection laws often require the retailer to accept a returned product, no questions asked. The company is then left with a refunded sale and a customer full of hate.

By too cold, I mean you're doing nothing to facilitate selling the customer what he or she wants. How many times have you gone into a big department store, found an item you'd like to buy, and then had to go searching for a clerk to ring you up? Or had people working the floor who were untrained, with little product knowledge? This was the classic mistake made by Circuit City in 2003, when in a cost-cutting move the company eliminated its skilled commissioned sales force. In one day, the company fired 3,900 of its highest-paid salespeople, with plans to replace them with 2,100 hourly associates. The move crushed employee morale and productivity, and left customers bewildered. In 2007, Circuit City laid off 3,400 more of the company's most experienced salespeople. The company essentially told its loyal customers, "You don't matter anymore. We'll take your hatepoints because we're trying to keep our shareholders happy until the next quarter."

The strategy was a massive failure. On November 10, 2008, Circuit City filed for Chapter 11 bankruptcy and soon thereafter, complete liquidation. At the time of the filing, Circuit City had 567 stores and about 34,000 employees nationwide, all of whom lost their jobs.

The soft sell is the happy medium. Be there for the customer. Be well informed and friendly. Remember the different customer types, and provide the type of service each one expects. Make the shopping experience a pleasure. Never seem desperate or pushy—but be truthful. Describe the capabilities and value of your product honestly. If you've got a car on your lot that was driven only on Sundays by a little old lady, then say so. If the car is an old beater, then say so, and price it accordingly.

Trust and transparency are the keys to collecting lovepoints and achieving long-term success.

TAKE ACTION!

The first touchpoints are critical, because this is when the prospect has the opportunity to base their judgment of the company on an actual interaction. It's imperative that your people are trained to recognize and interact with the four main types of customers: the Driver, the Analytical, the Amiable, and the Collaborator. Each persona includes adults of all ages, ethnicities, and gender identification. Your customer-facing people need to quickly identify which persona has approached them (or they are approaching), and instantly adapt to their personality.

CHAPTER 4

TOUCHPOINT #3:
THE CORE TOUCH

The goal of the sales funnel is to attract as many prospective customers as possible in the pre-touch stage, and entice them to enter the wide end for the first touch. There, they interact with the company and its products or services for the first time. They may browse the website, come into the store, or call on the phone. At every touch—and there may be many, especially in B2B settings, or with major consumer purchases such as a new car—you, the company, have an opportunity to score either lovepoints or hatepoints. Since we live in an imperfect world, it may not be possible to eliminate every hatepoint. It's the goal, but it could be achieved only in a perfect, frictionless market, which doesn't exist. It's your job to score as many lovepoints as possible while working to eliminate the hatepoints.

The core touch is the moment when the customer decides to purchase your product or service and is prepared to hand over her money or sign a contract. It extends to the delivery of the product.

THE DREADED CHECKOUT LINE

For owners of brick-and-mortar stores, the core touchpoint provides many opportunities to score both lovepoints and reduce
hatepoints. While e-commerce has severely disrupted (and in
some cases, including bookstores, utterly destroyed) the in-store
shopping experience, many consumers still enjoy it. A 2013 study
from Synqera reported in MediaPost found that more than
two-thirds of Americans still want to shop at traditional, brick-
and-mortar stores. However, one part of the brick-and-mortar
shopping experience was still riddled with hatepoints: Synqera
found the checkout process was the number one pain point for 73
percent of consumers, and was enough to make many of them
abandon the store and turn to online sites.[1]

The majority of consumers say waiting in the checkout line is
their least favorite part of in-store shopping. Here are some of the
most common hatepoints, and how they can be corrected.

- **The turtle in line ahead of you.** With customers growing
  increasingly used to ordering online with just a few clicks,
  waiting in line behind a slow-moving shopper can be
  exasperating. The hate grows when the person wants to
  pay with a paper check, and you stand there while they
  meticulously scribble. What can the store do? Don't
  scrimp on staff—make sure you have adequate cashiers on
  hand to deal with expected traffic volumes, and that your
  point-of-sale technology is up-to-date so it doesn't create
  a bottleneck. Also, many supermarkets are now offering
  self-checkout areas, where the customer can go at their
  own pace.

- **The turtle operating the cash register.** When you get to the register, you're greeted by a cashier who's changing the register tape or doing some other bit of housekeeping. In addition, some cashiers are just low-energy and slow in their movements. The solution is training! Remember, your competition isn't just the supermarket or retail store down the street, it's Amazon and Walmart online, which offer nearly frictionless checkout.

- **The invisible employees.** You're in a store and have a question, and you look around for a sales associate, and you see. . . . nobody. Your frustration builds as you search. You might even just walk out.

  If you operate a physical store, what separates you from the online retailers and other stores is your level of personal service. When a customer enters a store, he or she doesn't want to see a vast empty space. They want to see the floor staff ready to assist. They don't want to be ignored, but the opposite is also true—they don't want to be pounced upon and given a hard sell. Your floor staff should be alert and responsive, and be ready to provide the type of service the customer wants. Remember, some customers want to get in and out quickly. Others want to be friendly, and linger and chat. Others have lots of questions about the products, while others need to gather information and then go home and consult with their partner. By providing each with the service they want, you'll avoid hatepoints and pile up the lovepoints.

- **Being forced to play "checkout line roulette."** Customers at supermarkets and other big stores absolutely *hate* being forced to choose which checkout line they want to stand in. You know the feeling . . . you choose a line that looks like it's going quickly, but then the shopper in front of you turns out to be a turtle. You watch in dismay as shoppers who arrived after you are whisked through the checkout lines you didn't choose. The hatepoints pile up! The solution is to have a "one line for all registers" system, as most banks and airport check-in lines employ. Whether you're selling retail products or providing services, your customers just want to be treated quickly and fairly.

If you see a common thread in this discussion, you're right: 90 percent of the hatepoints in your physical store can be turned into lovepoints by *having a well-trained and robust human staff*. Human beings are social creatures, and we enjoy interacting with each other if the interactions are positive. Again, we go back to Walmart, the company everyone loves to hate but still succeeds year after year, decade after decade. From the beginning in 1962, Sam Walton instituted his "ten-foot rule," which took the form of a pledge: "I solemnly promise and declare that every customer that comes within ten feet of me, I will smile, look them in the eye, greet them, and ask if I can help them."

It's not easy, because human employees cost money. Currently, with 2.2 million people on its payroll, Walmart is the third-largest employer in the world, trailing only the US Department of Defense (3.2 million on the payroll) and the People's Liberation Army of China (2.3 million). Finding a way to save money on labor, or to eliminate jobs altogether, may be a huge boon to the retailer—but it has to remember that Walmart customers don't want to enter a vast box and not see any employees.

THE STORY OF THE HOTEL'S UNHAPPY CUSTOMERS

Let me give you just a quick example of the superpower of a hate-centric approach toward customer insights. I once worked with a luxury hotel group. Their surveys indicated that customers were complaining about the prices of the rooms. The hotel therefore concluded that their pricing was too high, and they reduced the base price of a room. After a few months, they did another survey—but to the hotel's surprise, customers still said the prices were too high. The hotel's leadership thought, "This is crazy—our prices are highly competitive with other luxury hotels!"

We decided that we would conduct a hate analysis to find out what customers were *specifically* hating. To our surprise, we found that the customers weren't concerned about the price in general. It was the *friction* involved in how the bill was presented.

When you checked into this hotel, the clerk would say, "Your room will be $322 per night."

Okay, fine.

"Plus a $15 valet charge."

All right.

"Plus a resort charge of $30."

A $30 "resort" charge? What is *that*? The hotel is downtown—nowhere near a resort!

"And also the cleaning fee, which is $50."

Wait, what? This was another new surprise the hotel added. You want me to pay to have my room cleaned?

Why were they doing this? My guess is that they did it in order to be able to *advertise* a lower rate, but still get the revenues they wanted! But this was not Motel Six, which caters to travelers who need to be careful about every penny they spend. This was a hotel that catered to wealthy people, and if there's one thing that wealthy people hate, it's being "nickel and dimed." The last thing they want is to be bothered with the details of the bill.

From what they *hate*, you can easily deduce what they *want*: a seamless entry into the lap of luxury, and no irritating conversations with desk clerks over the cost of having the room cleaned.

I suggested to the hotel that they offer *one flat price*. Include their so-called phony-baloney "resort fee." Include the "valet fee." And let's absolutely include the "room cleaning fee." Add them all into the base price to create a new price. That's what you'll advertise, and that's what the customer will expect to pay. Your customer doesn't need to know the breakdown of where each dollar goes on your expense spreadsheet. They don't care about that.

The hotel wisely took my advice. They raised the advertised prices and made the check-in and billing process much simpler. Sure enough, there were no more complaints about the price. Everybody was happy with the hotel.

At least that particular hotel learned a valuable lesson: stop annoying your well-heeled guests. But hotels do things like that all the time. How many times have you checked into a luxury hotel that charges $300 a night, gone to your room, and have seen a bottle of mineral water with a price tag on it that says ten dollars? Why didn't they just include that in the price of the room? It's doubly irritating because you know you could go outside, walk down the block to the nearest 7-Eleven store, and buy the same damn bottle for three dollars. To dig for incremental, microscopic amounts of new profit is a bad optic.

The real problem is we're really good at adding sources of new potential profit, like resort fees and overpriced mineral water. But we're really bad at seeing the impact of irritated customers who leave for disruptive innovators who deliver far better conspicuous value.

THE BIGGEST SOURCE OF HATEPOINTS: LYING TO YOUR CUSTOMER

Human beings are, by nature, trusting of each other. That may sound naïve, but it's true. We wouldn't have progressed over thousands of years to where we are today if we weren't able to work together and get things done cooperatively. And to do that, you need a baseline level of trust.

Any exchange of value requires trust. I need to know that what you want to sell me is what you say it is, and that it's not something fake or defective or poisonous. I look for honesty and fair value, and if I discover I've been cheated, the hatepoints will pile up quickly.

The worst thing you can do to a customer is lie to them, either about the product itself or the price you want to charge. We saw in the luxury hotel story that customers were not infuriated by the total price. If the clerk had said, "Your room is $417 per night, all inclusive," they would have likely handed over their credit cards without complaint. But the room was advertised at $322— nearly $100 less—and the hotel made up the difference by springing additional charges when the customer was standing there at the check-in desk. Lots of hatepoints there!

Bait and Switch

Traditionally, "bait and switch" meant a store would advertise a particular product at a certain price, and then when the customer would come looking for the product, the store would say, "Sorry, that one is sold out—but we have this other one, and it's only slightly more expensive." Today there are laws against that kind of blatant lying; bait-and-switch advertising is grounds for an action of common-law fraud, unjust enrichment, and sometimes breach of contract. It can also be a violation of the Consumer Fraud and Deceptive Business Practices Act.

As the Cornell Law School has noted, the concept of bait and switch extends to more transactions than just buying a product. It often includes contracts for services. A typical example would be:

- The seller represented in its proposal that they would provide certain specified employees or staff members when performing the services.

- The recipient relied on this representation of information when evaluating the proposal.

- It was foreseeable and probable that the employees or staff members named in the initial proposal would *not* be available to implement the contract work.

- Employees or staff members other than those specified in the proposal instead were or would be performing the services.[2]

In a simple example, you hire a law firm to work on your case, with the understanding that a senior partner will be doing the work—and then you discover you're meeting with a junior associate. Bring on the hatepoints!

INTRUSIVE DATA MINING

A friend of mine went into a car dealership because he wanted to test drive their new SUV. It was just a regular car showroom, not a high-end supercar dealer, like Ferrari or Bentley, where test driving a $500,000 vehicle might involve a careful approach.

In an auto dealership, you generally do not get to choose your salesperson unless you happen to know one and can ask for him or her by name. Salespeople work on rotation, and each salesperson takes their turn greeting the new prospect. Fred was approached by Mike. Fred told him that he wanted to take an SUV for a test drive. Ten minutes, tops. Fred expected Mike would take a copy of his driver's license—fair enough!—and he'd be on the road.

Mike asked Fred to sit down at one of those little desks that the salespeople have, and he put a long form in front of him. "Please just fill this out, and we'll be on our way," he said.

"What is this?" asked Fred.

"Oh, just some information we need."

Fred scanned the form. Name, address, how did he hear about the dealership, his income, other cars he owned, what credit cards he had . . .

"Excuse me," Fred said, "but this form looks like something I'd fill out to qualify for an auto loan. I'm nowhere near that stage! I'm comparing cars, and I just wanted to take an SUV for a quick test drive."

"Sorry, but I need you to fill out the form," said Mike.

"Is your manager here?" asked Fred. Like leaves falling from a tree in autumn, the hatepoints were piling up.

"Uh, yes . . . I'll get him," replied Mike. He disappeared. A few minutes later he came back with the manager, Bill. He glanced at the form. "Oh, I see we're practically neighbors," said Bill with a big grin. "I live just a few minutes from you."

"Why am I filling out this intrusive form just to take a test drive around the block?" asked Fred.

"Oh, the company wants us to do that," replied Bill, somewhat sheepishly. He turned to Mike. "I think we can make an exception. Okay?"

Mike shrugged. "Sure, no problem."

The event left Fred with a sour taste. Clearly Mike was a new guy who believed that he needed to stick to the company policy. Bill then undermined the company by waiving the policy. If the policy was important, why set it aside just because the customer lived in the same neighborhood? This made Fred think. What other special perks could Friends of Bill (FoB) get at the dealership?

Fred resented the dealership's blatant attempt to collect his personal data for some undefined purpose. He ended up buying a different SUV from another dealer.

Data mining has become a global mega-industry. It's all part of the global personal data market, which refers to digital information about consumers, broken down into four categories:

- **Digital engagement data.** Information about how consumers interact with a business's website, emails, mobile apps, paid ads, social media pages, and customer service routes.

- **Personal data.** Includes information such as address, age, gender, and even Social Security numbers, as well as non-personally identifiable information such as your IP address, web browser cookies, and device IDs, which both your mobile device and laptop have.

  Depending on the source, it may also include personal medical and financial data that has been sold or shared by a third party such as a healthcare provider.

- **Attitudinal data.** Encompasses metrics on purchase criteria, consumer satisfaction, product desirability, and more.

- **Behavioral data.** Includes transactional details such as purchase histories, product usage information (such as repeated actions), and qualitative data (mouse movement information).

Companies use a wide variety of collection methods and sources to capture and process customer data, with interest in types of data ranging from demographic data to behavioral data. Customer data can be collected in three ways: by directly asking customers (such as by the form Fred was asked to fill out at the auto dealership), by indirectly tracking customers, and by appending other sources of customer data to that of the company. Companies that sell personal information and other data to third-party sources have become commonplace. Once captured, this information regularly changes hands in a vast data marketplace of its own.

Most of this activity takes place behind the scenes, out of sight of the customer. Be careful that your customer does not view this as obtrusive, or you'll be rewarded with more hatepoints!

23andMe + GlaxoSmithKline = Hatepoints

In 2018, the DNA analysis company 23andMe announced it was accepting an investment of $300 million from the big pharmaceutical company GlaxoSmithKline. In return, the drug maker gained exclusive rights to mine 23andMe's customer data for "drug targets"—that is, possible ailments for which the company could develop new drugs. To industry analysts, the deal came as no surprise. For the previous three and a half years, 23andMe had been sharing insights gleaned from consented customer data with GSK and at least six other pharmaceutical and biotechnology firms. Offering access to customer information in the service of science has been 23andMe's business plan from the beginning. Since its founding in 2006, the company has amassed a huge collection of data from the millions of people who have submitted spit samples—and up to $199 each—in return for insights on their genes.

But many customers were still surprised and angry, unaware of the fate of the personal data they had handed to 23andMe when they had signed the company's lengthy and extremely dense consent forms. The piling up of hatepoints may have had an effect on the business's bottom line. In February 2020, Kendra T wrote for the Harvard Business School that 23andMe had laid off 14 percent of its workforce a month earlier due to a slowdown in sales of its genetic testing kits. (This was still in the pre-COVID-19 era.) As a possible cause of the slowdown, 23andMe CEO Anne Wojcicki cited privacy concerns. She believed that customers were feeling anxious about sharing genetic data due to the publicity about Facebook and other technology companies sharing customer data without consent.

It was possible that 23andMe's lagging sales represented something more specific to the company. Because it was not fully transparent with customers about its data sharing practices, customers perceived it would put their private genetic information at risk.

On the 23andMe consent forms, the use and sharing of de-identified customer data had been presented as being for research and scientific development. It was not clear to customers that their data would be bought by pharmaceutical companies until 23andMe publicly partnered with GlaxoSmithKline. The revelation caused many customers to balk at sharing their genetic data with 23andMe. While customers may have felt comfortable sharing information for objective scientific research, they may not have been pleased that 23andMe shared their data with a for-profit company.[3]

The answer? Don't fudge the truth with your customers. Sooner or later, they'll find out—and the payback will be expensive.

TAKE ACTION!

Here in the core touch moments, the sale is made. Money changes hands. The mission of the company has been fulfilled.

A lot can go wrong, which will produce a customer who may have bought your product or service but who is unhappy with the experience. Remember, just because your customer has made a purchase does not mean that he or she is 100 percent in love with your company, brand, or service. Pay particular attention to any elements of "fine print" in contracts or fulfillment issues that can ignite hate. And be sure that your salespeople are well trained and focused on customer happiness!

If appropriate, ask them to take a quick RealRatings survey to find out what they hated and loved about their transaction.

CHAPTER 5

TOUCHPOINT #4:
THE LAST TOUCHES

There are some cynical companies that believe once they've gotten your money, the game's over. The rest of it—particularly order fulfillment—is just a routine that should be accomplished with as little effort as possible.

Companies that seek to minimize hatepoints and build lovepoints across the entire customer journey see it quite differently. They know that there are two powerful reasons why providing an excellent customer experience at every touchpoint, including after the customer has paid, is beneficial for the company and its bottom line.

1. YOU NEED BRAND AMBASSADORS

You can spend millions of dollars on marketing and advertising, and get good results. You can also spend very little on making your customers deliriously happy, and get results that are equally good or even better.

Brand ambassadors are former and current customers who are happy with the company to the extent that they will go beyond being passively pleased to being actively vocal about their feelings.

A brand ambassador is a person who says to their friend, "I just bought a new Buick. Best car ever made. Drives like a dream!" It's the kid who will only wear Nike shoes to the local basketball court. It's the foodie who says, "Oh, you're going to Cincinnati? You've got to try Skyline Chili!" They give the company lots of lovepoints, and they distribute the love to their friends and colleagues.

They build brand awareness and build trust among customers and followers. One reason why word of mouth is so effective is that, every day, consumers are bombarded with commercial marketing messages and information. Who could possibly pay attention to all of it? They've learned to cut through the noise and ignore what they deem irrelevant—including your company's ads.

But choices need to be made, and consumers need reliable information about products and services. There's no better place to get that information than from their peers. According to Nielsen, only a third of consumers say they trust traditional ads. The preferred source of product information? Ninety-two percent are more inclined to believe people who are in their circles than direct messaging from a brand. In second place comes online consumer reviews, with 70 percent of global consumers surveyed online indicating they trust messages on this platform.[1]

It makes sense. If you want information about the quality and performance of a product, it's more logical to ask an objective user of the product rather than depending on the paid messaging from the brand itself.

Your employees can also be brand ambassadors, spreading lovepoints among their peers. Employees who are proud to work for your company will spread the word about your organization's core company values, its employee value proposition (EVP), and their own employee experience. As Influencer Marketing Hub revealed, employees are active on social media, and they talk about their work experience: 81 percent of Millennials share information about their company.[2] And *Entrepreneur* reported that social media content shared by employees gets eight times more engagement than content shared through the brand's own social channels and is shared twenty-five times more frequently. Leads through employee social networks convert seven times more often than any other leads.[3]

Before, during, and after the sale, be sure your customer has plenty of lovepoints to share. There is no more powerful marketing tool on earth than a happy brand ambassador.

2. YOU NEED REPEAT CUSTOMERS

It's axiomatic that it costs more to find a new customer than keep a current one. It's all about the conversion rate and its associated costs.

While conversion rates are volatile and vary by industry, most experts estimate that the average conversion rate is somewhere between 1 and 3 percent. That is to say, of one hundred prospective customers who experience a first-touch moment with your brand, no more than three will become paying customers. Meanwhile, you've spent money trying to attract and convert the other ninety-seven prospects who are not going to become your customers. At the end of the day, if you spent $100 trying to convert one hundred prospects, and you succeeded in selling to three of them, then your cost of new customer acquisition has been roughly $33 each.

On the other hand, a repeat customer has a chance of converting—that is, buying from you again—that's as high as 70 percent. This can increase up to 90 percent if your customer has bought from you not just once, but twice.

Repeat customers buy in two ways.

1. **They buy the same consumable product over and over again.** Think of toothpaste. You probably buy the same brand of toothpaste every month or so. Let's say you buy a new tube of Colgate toothpaste every month. Each purchase is $4. In a year, you'll spend $48. Over ten years, it'll be $480. What will the Colgate-Palmolive Company spend to make each sale to you? Zero dollars. Now multiply that by a million loyal repeat customers, and you're talking about real money.

   I know a man who buys a new Cadillac every two years. Walter trades in his old one and buys a new one for $50,000 or so. Just like that. The people at the dealership know him well, and they treat him like a king. They should build a shrine to him in the break room.

   While these two companies profit from your repeat business, as the months and years pass, they *must* ensure they give you no reason to hate them and every reason to love them. They need to keep the quality high and the price fair. They must live up to your expectations. They can never take your patronage for granted.

   Remember the Cadillac Cimarron, produced from 1982 to 1988? It was a low-cost piece of junk, and represented the nadir of the Cadillac brand. Loyal customers abandoned the marque in droves. Automotive journalist Dan Neil included the Cimarron in his 2007 list of "Worst Cars of All Time," writing, "Everything that was wrong, venal,

lazy, and mendacious about GM in the 1980s was crystal-
lized in this flagrant insult to the good name and fine customers of Cadillac."[4]

The venerable company limped along until 1998, when
it introduced the Escalade. The luxury SUV—big, powerful, and intimidating—encompassed everything drivers
had always loved about the Cadillac brand and set the
company back on the road to success. The lesson for Cadillac—and for every company—was this: *Don't forget why
your customers love you. Stake out your turf, claim it, and
defend it. Don't imitate—innovate.*

2. **They buy your new products.** The person who buys Colgate toothpaste is likely to buy Colgate mouthwash and a
   Colgate toothbrush. My friend who buys a new Cadillac
   every year is interested in the new all-electric Cadillac
   Lyriq. Heck, as soon as the Lyriq hits the streets, the company should just give him one. (They probably won't go
   that far. But the dealer will make sure that Walter is among
   the very first customers to be invited for a test drive.)

   People who work in the arts—such as book authors,
   filmmakers, video gamers, and musicians—are keenly
   aware of the power of repeat customers to either make
   them or break them. How many musicians have put out
   two or three hit records and have built a solid fan base of
   repeat customers, and then released a couple of stiffs, only
   to see their customer base evaporate? Repeat customers
   do not represent a *guarantee* of continued lovepoints; they
   represent the *opportunity* to keep earning them.

• • •

THE CUSTOMER WILL RENDER THEIR VERDICT

The last-touch moments determine if you get to keep your customer. In other words, your customer will decide how easy and beautiful it is to do business with you.

If you're a wireless carrier, when compared to the competition, how are your plans evolving to maintain value and freedom from friction?

If you're a restaurant, do you remember your customers and engage with them?

If you're a car dealership, is your service department delivering friction-free and beautiful experiences? (That's a tough one! The vast majority of dealer service departments are *hated* by their customers. Ninety percent of car owners would rather take their in-warranty car to their local mechanic than back to the dealership. I have a friend who calls his dealer's service department the House of Satan. That's pretty bad.)

The core touchpoint is the bread and butter of customer experience. You have to institutionalize a culture of stakeholder and customer happiness and all of the mechanical aspects will fall into place.

JOLT THE EXPERIENCE WITH SHOCKING GOODNESS

The last touch moment is too often overlooked, and it's unfortunate that organizations do not take this moment seriously. This is where you leave the customer with a shockingly good experience or value.

Examples of great last touch moments include:

The Jacuzzi company that leaves you with a beautiful gift basket of all the chemicals and tools you need to maintain your Jacuzzi.

The automotive dealer that pulls your new car out on a red carpet and takes a picture of you with your car for you to share on your social channels. This dealer also provides a branded automotive care duffel bag chock-full of everything you could ever need to maintain your shiny new car.

The doctor who calls you a few hours after your visit to see how you're doing.

The luxury hotel that offers you a limo ride to the airport after you check out.

The pediatrician who hands you a copy of her book on raising healthy babies because you're one of her valued patients.

As you can see, these last touchpoints are incredibly memorable and relatively inexpensive to deploy; and they will provide you more referral business and customer retention than any phony-baloney CRM system or survey ever will. Make the last touch moment amazing, and your customer will lavish you with lovepoints.

REWARD YOUR LONG-TERM CUSTOMERS

Let's go back to the hard math of the cost of acquiring a new customer. I gave the example of spending $100 to try to convert a group of one hundred prospects. Three became customers, which meant that we spent about $33 to convert each one. Fortunately, our profit margin allows us to make some profit even though we spend $33 to acquire each new customer. Theoretically, we could stay in business only with new customers.

But repeat customers are so much more profitable! And because we have loyal repeat customers, it's tempting to spend nothing to get them. It's like free money!

Here's the problem: repeat customers aren't dummies. They know how the system works, and they expect special treatment. They want to be rewarded for their continued patronage.

This is why we should not use the formula of $33 to get a new customer vs. zero dollars to keep a repeat customer. If we do, we're living in a fool's paradise. Instead, our formula should be something like $33 to get a new customer vs. $20 to keep an existing customer. If we spend $20 to keep the existing customer, we're still $13 ahead.

How do we spend $20 on an existing customer? Through a rewards program. There are many ways you can regularly reward your repeat customers. Here are just a few, courtesy of Shopify:

- Designer Shoe Warehouse (or DSW) rewarded customers with points for each purchase and included tiers of rewards that customers could unlock as they spent more. Their program ran seamlessly—the online system recognized customers by their name, phone number, or payment information.

- Sephora's Beauty Insider rewards program boasted more than seventeen million loyal members, who earned rewards for each purchase based on a traditional point system. The innovative part was that members could choose how to use their reward points, for things such as gift cards and discounts.

- In the same vein, outdoor gear retailer The North Face had its VIPeak program in which loyalty points could be redeemed not just for merchandise but for special offers like attending The North Face events and participating in unique travel experiences, such as a mountain climbing adventure in Nepal.

- Cosmetic and skincare retailer Tarte used their loyalty program to incentivize user-generated content and social media engagement. Customers could earn rewards points not just by buying products but for activities like posting a selfie with Tarte products, writing online reviews, and posting video tutorials—transforming them into brand ambassadors.

- TOMS shoes rewarded its customers with points for every interaction, including just signing up for their email list. Then, when the customer amassed enough points, they could use them the usual way, or could apply them to one of various causes supported by the company, such as the One for One shoe donation and profit-sharing with causes like the Wildlife Conservation Society.

- Airline reward programs have been around for years. You fly on the airline, and you get air mile points or frequent flyer miles. You accumulate a set amount of miles based on how much you spend on a ticket or how much you spend on your credit card. You can then use these miles to buy more tickets. These programs work so well that people plan their flights—even their vacations—for maximum frequent flyer miles leverage.

- Amazon Prime—the king of all loyalty programs—offered unlimited free two-day shipping on millions of items, as well as other perks Amazon added like their streaming service and Prime Day sales, for a flat annual fee. And it worked—Prime members spent an average of four times more than other Amazon customers.

All of these programs require an investment by the company—but they all pay for themselves many times over with high customer loyalty and boosted sales.

THE VALUE OF NEGATIVE FEEDBACK

One last thing . . . During the last touch moment, there is an opportunity to ask, in a non-scripted, authentic way, "How was your experience with us?" Most organizations will never do this because they really don't want to know, and of the ones that do, many will never listen to the answer.

An effective way to find out is by asking it this way: "How could we have improved your experience with us?" The question is worded so that the customer infers you're looking for problem areas and you want to know the truth. This is your opportunity to find out if there are any hatepoints rattling around that you can immediately pluck out. Many of my clients have developed a system that asked this question, and if there were anything derogatory of any kind, they wanted to hear it!

Look at it this way: As the customer walks out the door, you ask them, "How was your experience today?"

Let's say they answer, "Just perfect, thank you!"

What does that tell you? Very little, actually. Remember the various types of customer personalities—the Driver, the Analytical, the Amiable, and the Collaborator—and the experiences they expect? It's unlikely that if you have eighty customers enter your store, with twenty of each type, that every single one of them will report a "perfect" experience. It's much more useful to learn about what you can improve, rather than be told that everything is perfect.

Negative feedback is a gift, because it's a key driver of performance and leadership effectiveness. Criticism is valuable because it allows us to honestly evaluate our performance and alerts us to important changes we need to make. Being alerted to mistakes and receiving suggestions for improvement does more to raise performance than positive feedback and praise.

COMCAST:
A TRANSFORMATION FROM HATE TO LOVE

Everyone makes mistakes. Companies are owned and operated by human beings, and inevitably a salesperson is going to do something offensive, or a manager will make a dumb, thoughtless decision. A customer service representative will be rude, or a social media manager will post an offensive Tweet. Any of these offenses, and many more, could alienate a stalwart long-term customer or even an entire class of customers.

For example, consider the cable giant Comcast. For years, its customer service operation was legendarily awful. It ranked as one of the most hated brands in the country. According to the 2015 American Customer Satisfaction Index report, Comcast ranked third from the bottom on pay television and dead last as an internet service provider. That made it among the most poorly rated companies in the two lowest-ranking categories.

In popular culture, "the cable guy" was such an icon of horrible service that it inspired a Hollywood feature film. Directed by Ben Stiller and starring Jim Carrey and Matthew Broderick, *The*

Cable Guy, released in 1996, reveled in the loathing that most customers felt toward the customer service arms of big cable companies including Comcast.

In one notable case from July 2014, Comcast's terrible customer service made headlines when one of its representatives kept a customer captive on the phone for about eighteen minutes, demanding to know why the household was choosing another cable provider. The customer happened to be Ryan Block, cofounder of tech site Engadget. He and his wife were moving and called to close their account. When the call turned nasty, Block began to record it.

After being interrogated for several minutes, Block said, "This phone call is a really actually amazing representative example of why I don't want to stay with Comcast. So can you please cancel our service?"

During the call, the customer service rep revealed the root of the problem when he said to Block, "My job is to have a conversation with you about keeping your service, about finding out why it is you're looking to cancel the service." To be more precise, the job of the customer service rep was to bully the customer to keep the service.

Much to the chagrin of Comcast, Block had eighty thousand Twitter followers, and after he posted the recording, it went viral on the internet. According to Soundcloud.com, by September 2014 it had been listened to more than five million times.[5]

Let that number sink in for a moment. *One* bad customer service call was heard *five million times* by current and potential customers.

After the story broke, a Comcast spokeswoman provided the following statement to ABC News about the call: "We are very embarrassed by the way our employee spoke with Mr. Block, and are contacting him to personally apologize. The way in which our representative communicated with him is unacceptable and not consistent with how we train our customer service representatives."[6]

In reality, it was probably *exactly* how the phone reps were trained.

Six months later, Lisa Brown had a similar experience that went viral. A volunteer for a missions organization in Spokane, Washington, in February 2015, Brown attempted to cancel her Comcast cable service after her family was experiencing financial difficulties. Instead of immediately canceling her service, Brown's call was escalated to a "retention specialist," who tried to cajole her into signing a new two-year contract.

Brown was able to eventually cancel her service, but on her final billing statement she noticed a shocking surprise: her husband's name had been changed from "Ricardo Brown" to "Asshole Brown"! The insult surfaced, and Comcast was forced to make amends. "We have spoken with our customer and apologized for this completely unacceptable and inappropriate name change," Steve Kipp, Comcast's vice president of communications for the Washington region, told Elliott.org, which had investigated the story. "We have zero tolerance for this type of disrespectful behavior and are conducting a thorough investigation to determine what happened."[7]

Many more stories like these made Comcast one of the worst-rated companies for customer service.

Then a miracle happened: the company turned itself around.

One major step was the creation of a new position in the company. In September 2014, Comcast announced the appointment of Charlie Herrin to the role of senior vice president of customer experience—or CXO, for customer experience officer. He was given broad powers to fix Comcast's hate-filled relationship with its customers and oversight of over more than fifty call centers and tens of thousands of customer service employees and technicians.

It's worth quoting what Tom Karinshak, Comcast's executive vice president of customer service, told Micah Solomon from *Forbes* in November 2017. "Here's what I know for certain," said Karinshak. "We needed to *do* better. We needed to *be* better. We needed to reimagine a whole new experience for the customer, and not just fix the one we have. We took a look at everything—from our culture, training, systems, processes, technology, and tools—to create a fundamentally better customer and employee experience. Because to be successful, *it all starts with our employees.*" (I added the emphasis.) He added, "We're using an inside out approach, beginning with the employee experience. Again, you can't have a great customer experience without a great employee experience."[8]

Comcast also introduced accountability. The company knew its customers *hated* the vague, three-hour window for in-home service calls, which forced customers to wait at home for the cable guy to show up. The company offered one- to two-hour appointment windows and, even better, introduced Tech ETA, which proactively messaged the customer when their technician would arrive, through their mobile phone or on their TV screen. (To be honest, given today's advanced GPS technology, this should be a no-brainer to implement.) But the company backed up its promise with the guarantee that if the technician was even one minute late for an appointment, the customer would get $20 off their next bill.

The company introduced Xfinity Assistant, a cross-channel, virtual customer-service tool. Xfinity Assistant answers customers' questions around the clock without them needing to stop what they're doing to call customer service reps. "At Comcast, we see millions of interactions happening every day with our customers," the company said in a press release. "The need for simple, digital solutions has never been more important, and our multi-year investment in digital platforms and capabilities are paying off."[9]

In addition, Comcast has developed a sophisticated program for collecting and evaluating customer experience feedback. As Karinshak explained to CXOTalk, one component was called Sentiment, which measured the overall satisfaction from all customer touchpoints, whether they're written or voice-related. "It takes into account everything that we're hearing from the customers that way," he said. "We can go beyond just sampling customers, like what you get sometimes with the surveys, to accounting for all of their transactions. Then we couple that customer, that employee feedback with our own business insights and intelligence that we're seeing as well, too, and we garner that."[10]

Karinshak then added something rather astonishing for a huge company with millions of customers. He said, "Everybody in the company does callbacks talking to customers directly, [including] our senior leaders like myself and others. I'll stick with CEO Dave Watson as an example. He'll share his feedback that he has gotten directly from talking to customers to us and talking to employees to us through roundtables or other things. It really is woven into the fabric [of the company]."[11]

At its growing number of physical stores—in 2018, Comcast opened over eighty stores in high-traffic retail areas versus their traditional industrial locations of the past—they call their customer-facing employees "Friendly Experts," who are trained to execute on three behaviors:

1. **Warm welcome.** (This is taking a cue from the age-old maxim promulgated by Sam Walton.)

2. **Own it.** (Take responsibility for your ability to please or displease the customer. The buck stops with you.)

3. **Show appreciation in each customer interaction.** (You need to proactively inform your customer that you are there to serve them and are grateful for their patronage.)

In June 2020, the American Customer Satisfaction Index released the results of its annual, wide-ranging survey gauging consumers' feelings about their telecom services. The survey found Comcast's Xfinity brand was the "most improved" overall, and especially saw a "staggering improvement" in satisfaction with its pay TV service. The Xfinity retail stores, which the company has overhauled in recent years to have a more high-tech, boutique-like setting, also saw a big jump in score. "According to customers, Xfinity staff are making a difference as in-store transaction speed is the most-improved factor of the customer experience," the report stated.[12]

Comcast is a good example of a company that was hated by its own customers, then saw the problem, owned the problem, and took a massive, company-wide effort to change the hate into love. It's not rocket science. It's all about having the fortitude to embrace innovation, inspire your employees, and do the right thing for your customers.

TAKE ACTION!

After the sale is made, you need to think about two things: your customer as a brand ambassador, spreading the good word about your company, brand, or service; and your customer becoming a repeat buyer who comes back time and time again.

Identify and correct any and all sources of hate at this stage. Take heart in knowing that no matter how much your customers hate your company—like the way they hated Comcast in the 1990s and well into the 21st century—it's never too late to stage an intervention and get on the right track. Remember that innovation needs to play an important part, because customers have increasingly powerful and immediate ways of voicing their love or hate for your company.

CHAPTER 6

TOUCHPOINT #5:
THE IN-TOUCH

During the in-touch stage, while the immediate sale may have been concluded and the product or service delivered, your customer hasn't fallen off the face of the earth. On the contrary, he or she may be active in the marketplace for years and even decades to come, as will your company (we hope!).

THE BIG CIRCLE

In a sense, an established customer to whom you sold something in the past has come full circle, and has returned to the vast pool of prospective customers who hover just beyond the entrance to your sales funnel. There the customer lingers, ready to enter the sales funnel again when they have a need or desire that your company can fulfill. Good examples of such periodic businesses would be your local auto repair shop, wedding venue, plumber, mortgage lender, hospital, or hotel—any business you might patronize on a semi-regular basis.

There are two very important differences between a cold prospect with whom you have never done business and a former customer who may return.

1. **The relationship.** Your former customer has the positive memory of the transaction, and doesn't need to be educated about what you can do for them. They'll need far less persuading than a new customer. They have your product and love it. (If they don't, then you've got a host of really bad problems.) In a sense, they are yours to lose.

2. **Their data.** You have a record of their interactions with you. If you're an online retailer like Amazon, this data will be highly detailed, and will include their complete shopping and browsing history. The browsing data gives the online retailer a significant advantage over the physical retailer, because the physical store has no way of recording the items you looked at but didn't buy. For example, if you go to a department store and spend ten minutes looking at microwave ovens in the kitchenware department and don't buy one, and then you go and buy a pair of sneakers, the department store has *no record* of your interest in microwave ovens. None whatsoever. But if you go online and spend ten minutes looking at microwave ovens before buying a pair of sneakers, the online retailer knows that in addition to buying a pair of sneakers, you also had a very keen interest in microwave ovens, but for some reason you didn't find what you were looking for. Their response will be to target you with pop-up ads for both shoes and microwave ovens.

Your shopping data can be used to predict what you might want to buy (Amazon uses algorithms to suggest products to its customers) and to make the next purchase friction-free.

With a former customer, this is what you're starting with, and it's a huge advantage over what you need to do to reel in a cold prospect.

Having said that, your former customer's or repeating customer's continuing relationship to your company may take one of many forms.

REPEAT BUYER

As I mentioned in the previous chapter, your onetime customer may become a repeat customer who buys your product regularly. This is the person who is loyal to one brand of toothpaste, or one automobile, or one income tax service. They are happy with your products or services, and as long as you keep the lovepoints high and the hatepoints very low, you're likely to keep them. Being your customer is efficient for them. After all, changing brands involves some risk and adjustment, and most consumers have better things to do than constantly approach each routine purchase as if it were totally new.

In their case, you *never* want to subject them to a hard sell. The minimum you must do is ensure they feel good about choosing your brand, always deliver quality, and beware of competitors who would poach your loyal customers.

Sadly, some marketing directors believe they need to stay in touch with their customers by constantly spamming them with emails and self-serving offers. Customer relationship management (CRM) software packages are often used to stay in touch for the purpose of getting customers to buy something else. But this isn't what customers love; it's often what they *hate*. Instead, deliver ongoing constant value. Let your customers know about special offers only if you know it's something they need to have.

CROSS-BUYER

You go to your favorite burger joint and place your order.

The server says, "Do you want to try our new Cajun French fries with that?"

"Uh, yes, sure," you reply.

You've just experienced *cross-selling*, which is encouraging the purchase of a secondary or new product in conjunction with the primary product. In this example, the primary product was a burger, which you've had many times, and your server asked if you wanted to try their new Cajun French fries.

A master of cross-selling new products to existing customers is Apple. The company began in 1976 with a personal computer, the Apple I. In 1993 they brought out the Newton Message Pad, and in 2001 the iPod music player. Then in 2007 came the iPhone, and in 2015 the Apple Watch. Each of these new products was initially sold to existing Apple customers, so that if you were a loyal Apple user, you might very well own a computer, music player, phone, and even the watch.

Cross-buyers are the consumers who love the *Star Wars* movies, so they buy all the *Star Wars* merchandise, too. They like the Kardashians, so they buy whatever the family is selling. They like their Ford pickup truck, so they buy all the aftermarket accessories to make it special.

A distinction should be made between cross-selling and upselling.

- **Cross-selling** occurs when you sell customers offerings that complement or supplement the purchases they've already made. For example, if you encourage a customer who just bought a new music player to get a set of headphones, that's cross-selling. Cross-selling can happen long after the initial sale—for example, you download a new video game, and then the company puts out a feature film version a few years later, and you're first in line to see it.

  Typically, if you avoid the hard sell, you won't get hatepoints for trying to stay in touch. Your communications with your former customer must be reasonable, not pushy, and feel less like an advertisement and more like information being shared.

- **Upselling** occurs when you increase a customer's value by encouraging them to pay for additional services or purchase a more expensive model. For example, if someone comes into your furniture store looking for a chair and you sell them the entire dining room set instead, that's an upsell. Generally, upselling happens at the time of the purchase. The seller in effect says, "Hey, if you're already spending $10 with us and you're happy, then why not spend $15 and be even more happy?"

Restaurants are often very good at upselling. They have a captive audience—you're sitting at the table—and you both know you're going to spend *some* money. The only question is *how much*. Your skilled server will offer a steady stream of suggestions—"How about some drinks before you order? The filet mignon is very good tonight. What can I get you for dessert? Coffee or a cordial?" Before you know it, you've jacked up your "ticket"—the total bill per person—and increased the restaurant's margins.

At a restaurant, customers usually enjoy being upsold, as long as it's done gently. But you need to be extremely careful when upselling, because your customer can easily feel used. Too much upselling can lead to massive hatepoints—for example, it's why so many people are leery of real estate agents. You tell the real estate agent that you're looking for a two-bedroom house for $400,000, and the first house they show you is a three-bedroom for $500,000! Pile on the hatepoints! The same goes for new car dealers, who, when you've said you're going to buy the car, make you sit at the manager's desk and review, one by one, the endless list of optional features and services you can buy. They know you *hate* it—but they also know that the average customer will agree to one or more of the upsell items on the list, which from their point of view makes the torturous process worthwhile.

INFLUENCER

Even if your customer never buys a single thing from you ever again, they'll always remember their relationship with you and, when the occasion arises, relate their experience—good or bad—to a friend or family member. This makes your customer an influencer, and good ones are worth their weight in gold.

A friend of mine and his partner once had to move into a hotel near their home. Let's call it Hotel Diamond. They were having work done on their house, and so for two weeks they lived at the hotel, just as any tourists would. They had a lovely experience and, after the two weeks ended, they moved back home.

Hotel Diamond put them on the hotel's email list. Every month or so, my friend got an email from the hotel announcing a special event or some improvement, like a new workout center or improved Wi-Fi. The emails weren't sales pitches; they were more like friendly newsletters.

Of course, my friend and his partner were probably never going to patronize that hotel again. It was only a few miles from their house—there was no point in going there! But my friend knew a lot of people, including those who would fly into the city for business or family visits. On a regular basis, they would ask for his advice on finding a good hotel. Invariably, he would tell them to stay at the one they had used while their house was being remodeled—the Hotel Diamond.

Over the following five years, my friend referred a dozen or more high-value, out-of-town friends and relatives to the Hotel Diamond. Eventually the hotel's general manager noticed, and so he invited my friend and his partner to stay for a weekend, all expenses paid. My friend's relationship with Hotel Diamond turned out to be immensely beneficial for both parties, long after my friend had stopped being a paying customer.

LET'S STAY CONNECTED

It's important to stay connected with your customers after their experience with you has ended. You must approach this with an absolute commitment not to sell them anything, but rather to consistently and pleasantly provide them with ongoing value. You want them to willingly come back to you of their own accord, not because you're shoving some "One time only!" shenanigans down their throats.

You have probably had the experience of moving at some point in your life, and ultimately losing touch with the friends and family you left behind. In business, in order to maintain a relationship, you need to commit to regular and valuable engagement. This ordinarily takes the form of newsletters or emails that highlight an innovation within the industry or the company.

The purpose of your in-touch moment engagement strategy is to provide ongoing and continuous value to your customer even if they are no longer technically a customer. I used to work with a large digital agency, and one day they called to tell me about a new marketing opportunity that would be a fit for my firm. This wasn't a marketing opportunity that they provided; they just felt that they could really benefit me, and they wanted to let me know about it. I kept waiting for the "gotcha," but there wasn't one. They just wanted to add continuous value to me, and I appreciated it. So much, in fact, that I decided to refer them to one of my biggest clients, which resulted in a sale for their firm worth a quarter of a million dollars. Staying in touch isn't just about increasing revenue, although it certainly can do that; it's about making certain you have the continuity of a contiguous line of value that you deliver to your customer.

Many organizations are *losing* significant amounts of revenue and an opportunity to do a far better job of serving their customer by eliminating the work that needs to be done in the in-touch moment.

THE CUSTOMER JOURNEY CONTINUUM AND THE WEAKEST LINK

As the axiom suggests, the strength of a chain is only as good as its weakest link. Many organizations are exceptional at one or more of the various touchpoints. The challenge is you have to be good at each and every touchpoint to both build up the love and eliminate what customers hate across all of your customers' personas. A fractional approach toward customer journey mapping and design will be incredibly ineffective. So many great leaders—and, for that matter, great companies—have failed just because they took their eye off one of the touchpoints.

YOU NEED LOVEPOINTS FROM YOUR EMPLOYEES, TOO!

We know now how important a first touch moment is, so how do we eliminate the things that customers hate? Let me give you an example of some of the many things that have been covered in my years as a management consultant working with organizations to help them optimize their customer experience.

I worked with a national fast-food restaurant franchise to help them identify what customers hated about them. Specific to the first touchpoint, when a customer would walk into the restaurant, the person behind the counter would not even acknowledge them. Too many times, the customer service person just stared at the customer, with a neutral or even derogatory facial expression, waiting for the customer to read the overhead menu and give their order. In other words, you would walk into this restaurant and they would stare at you as if to say, "What do *you* want?" It was literally that bad.

The disdain for the customer was systemic. But why? Were these employees born rude, or did they get that way?

More digging and interviewing revealed, perhaps not surprisingly, that the restaurant was far from a happy workplace. The employees were not mean people, but they were miserable in their jobs. The restaurant owners and managers lacked any capacity for leading a workforce, and treated their employees with deep suspicion, as if they were all potential criminals. Sexist jokes were common, and any employee who came in with a backpack could expect it to be searched before they went home. Scheduling was erratic and overtime was mandatory.

Not surprisingly, employee turnover was very high, as employees worked there only long enough to get relevant job experience that they could take elsewhere. Meanwhile, the only new recruits were kids who couldn't get a job anywhere else. It was a vicious downward spiral, with the owners lamenting they couldn't find quality employees—but the ones they had, they drove away with hate!

To solve their employee problem, the restaurant owners then experimented by replacing their angry workforce with automated kiosks. The experiment confirmed that customers did indeed prefer a kiosk over an unhappy worker. Therefore, the organization concluded that they could fix their problems by simply digitizing the ordering process. But wait—did they really fix the problem? No! *They solved the wrong problem* and increased what people really hated.

Meanwhile, down the street, competing fast-food restaurants were implementing quality-of-work-life programs, thoughtful hiring and onboarding processes, and a wide range of human approaches toward their employees. These efforts made the employees happier, and they in turn treated the customers with courtesy and respect.

To this story, there are two morals:

1. **Your employees are your frontline brand ambassadors.** As human beings, they will transfer their emotions

to other employees or, if they're sales associates, to your customers. Whether your sales associate is an executive working with million-dollar clients or a kid standing behind the counter of your pizza place, he or she needs to enjoy their work. They need to be able to take pride in their work.

Who knows—your entry-level employee might just be the next Jay Leno. Before finding fame and fortune as an entertainer, Leno started his career with a minimum wage job at a McDonald's in Andover, Massachusetts. "I worked at a restaurant on Main Street for two years, from 1966 to 1968," Leno told author Cody Teets in *Golden Opportunity: Remarkable Careers That Began at McDonald's*. While slicing potatoes for French fries and ringing up customers at McDonald's, Leno learned a lesson about business that stuck with him throughout his career.

One morning, while preparing to cut potatoes, Leno walked back to the restaurant's storage room to grab a new batch. Tom Curtin, the owner/operator, was with him. The two men noticed something unusual: there, on top of the sack of potatoes, was a pair of underwear.

"Sometimes crew members changed into their uniforms at work, and somebody had apparently forgotten their underpants," Leno said. "I expected Tom to tell me to throw out the top layer of potatoes and wash the rest. Instead, he said simply, 'Get rid of all those potatoes. Get rid of that whole batch. Just get rid of all of it.'"

"That was very impressive to me," Leno remembered. "The standards for quality were quite high. It was one of those life lessons I never forgot."[1]

Indeed, Curtin's message to his young employee was very clear: Our customers deserve the very best we can give them. We're interested in eliminating hatepoints and increasing lovepoints, from the manager to the employee to the customer.

2.   **Never try to fix a first-touch hatepoint with a solution that can only be described as "We Suck Less."** This will result in certain failure. Instead of confronting the problem of employee management and training, an action that would have required them to examine their own attitudes and beliefs, the owners of the fast-food restaurant swept the problem under the rug. They decided to get rid of as many of the troublesome human employees as possible and make the business not only fast-food but self-service. Why was this stupid? Because when customers go to an automat, they expect the food to be cheap and ubiquitous. (Remember, a successful business is all about correctly gauging customer expectations and then meeting or exceeding them.) Automat food is just stuff you eat because you're in such a hurry that you can't even slow down for fast food! How do you make money with an automat? The only way is through massive volume, both in the number of sales you make and the number of low-priced products you sell.

As you can see, the fast-food owners made a decision that effectively took their business out of one industry (fast food) and into another (automats), thereby creating a new set of problems for themselves. They jumped from a hot frying pan into a much hotter fire!

TO KEEP THE LOVE COMING, EMBRACE DISRUPTION!

Every time I've seen a company identify its most profitable customers and place most of its resources there, I've found that these customers were the most profitable because they were subscribing to what that company was doling out.

But how about making nonprofitable customers profitable? Understand your customers across all your customer types. Walk around, be disruptive, and look at what you can create that's new and relevant by looking at what you can destroy. This is the best way to come up with disruptive ideas and turn nonprofitable customers into profitable ones.

TAKE ACTION!

After the sale is complete, your customer returns to the vast pool of prospects. But now you have a positive history with them, and if they want to buy again, yours is the sale to lose. Your job is to stay in touch with them, and not by harassing them with sales pitches but by sending them news and offers. Make them "part of the family," but keep it low key.

Ensure your employees are fully engaged, know the organization's mission, and are happy to be at work every day. You cannot possibly drive down the hatepoints if your employees are the source of them!

CHAPTER 7

STOP FOCUSING ONLY ON WHAT YOU THINK CUSTOMERS WANT

I know that sounds crazy! I mean, after all, creating new experiences and products and services, and beautifully delivering those to customers in a way that they want, is absolutely the critical aspect of what it means to deliver an exquisite customer experience. But it turns out that if we focus *only* on what customers want, as many organizations do, we're operating from the assumption that their current state of customer experience is acceptable.

The post-COVID economy is a time of hyper-competition and hyper consumerization. Customers demand complete freedom from friction. They want price transparency. They want every transaction to be seamless. So if we assume that our current business model and the way in which we deliver value in every possible way—from the quality of our products, to our product packaging, to our distribution and supply chain methods, to everything—are all okay, and now we just need to find out what our customers want, we won't get where we need to be.

THE BAR KEEPS GETTING HIGHER

A few years ago, I started asking my clients the question "What do your customers hate about you?" This was after I had been talking to their customers, and had heard some eye-opening opinions, and now I wanted to ask the company itself. Wow, this was an incredible moment. I discovered something that was exceptionally powerful. Not only did customers tell me all the things they hated about dealing with a particular company, but the same company's employees also told me all the things they *knew* their customers hated! One company in particular had just spent $18 million in a marketing campaign, yet they never spent a dime on asking the fundamental question, "What do our customers hate about us? And how can we fix that?"

Right now, the overwhelming majority of your customers are receiving what I call the *baseline level of current expectation*. In other words, you're giving them what you think they want. The problem is, in a time of massive change, the bar continues to rise, and customers are wanting far more than they used to. They want to be surprised with exquisite experiences and value. Organizations operating in that danger zone of the baseline level of current expectation are likely going to fail—maybe tomorrow, maybe next year, but ultimately, that danger zone is real. And it's what's killed many of the best organizations on the planet. So let's think about why we would ask ourselves the question "What do our customers hate?" as being just as important as "What do our customers love?" And that's the thesis of this program. I discovered that so much information can be gleaned when you look at the flip side of the coin. In other words, if you find out what a customer hates, then they've just told you what they want in a clear and crisp way.

EVERYONE LOOKS FOR THE
ONE-STAR RATINGS

A powerful reason why it's extremely important to think about the haters as much as the lovers is that haters can cause revenue and customer defection. In a time of digital ubiquity, and what Google refers to as "micro mobile moments," we use our connected devices to make decisions about where we go to dinner, what hotels we stay in, and what products we're going to buy. And one of the ways in which we make those decisions is what we call *hyper influential social communities*. For an example, on Amazon, when you're thinking about buying a product, the first thing you're likely to do is find out how other consumers rated the product. The larger the crowd, the more authentic the rating is, so you take a look at the ratings. Now, let me ask you a really simple question: Like me, and virtually everybody else, do you skip all of the five-star ratings and go straight to the one-star rating? We do that because we want to know what the haters think. If something is wrong with the product, we'll find out by reading the bad reviews. The haters are some of the most influential customers we have. Isn't that interesting? The people who hate what we do have the biggest influence over our success.

The solution is to stop making customers hate us. Get rid of the one-star reviews.

But wait, how do we do that? Find out what customers *hate*. Seems pretty simple. But it's interesting to me that virtually every discussion on the topic of customer experience has to do with trying to find out what customers want. And the truth of the matter is, customers really don't know what they want. And you know what? It's not their job to invent a better experience. That's *your* job. That's where the heavy lifting comes in. I know surveys and promoter scores and other tools are fun. They create great graphs and charts. They're easy to use. They're supposed to be best practice, but really understanding the haters is the secret to developing the best customer experiences on the planet.

HATERS WILL DEFLECT YOUR CUSTOMERS

The pop star Taylor Swift famously said in one of her top songs, "The haters are gonna hate." But here's the bigger problem with haters: they're *deflectors*.

What do I mean by that? I mean that they will destroy your business if you don't know them and fix the hate.

There's something called the "bumper sticker syndrome." Have you ever noticed that the people with the worst ideas have the most bumper stickers? Well, it turns out that haters are very prolific, and they are loud. Haters have big voices. I call haters part of the "loud crowd." And the loud crowd can't wait to talk about how much they hate you.

Now, don't get me wrong, but in our world there are plenty of trolls. There are negative, destructive people who just want to say something bad about somebody else. But generally speaking, the data that comes in and the rating aggregation of the trolls are usually not statistically meaningful. Every business has its share of trolls.

The point that I'm trying to make here is that your genuine, sincere haters have the power to deflect business from you. If your social ratings are low because customers hate you, and you have not resolved those hatepoints, then you will ultimately fail. We cannot afford what we now call digital deflection. But it's not just there that we get deflected; we can be deflected anywhere along the customer touchpoints. And understanding what customers hate is far more insightful than knowing the praise customers tell you.

The moral of the story here is pretty straightforward. If we really want to know what customers want, we have to first of all look at the flip side of the coin, which is what they hate. That's where they tend to speak far more accurately.

When it comes to what customers really want, it's our responsibility to create that. It never showed up on a survey at Apple that Steve Jobs should have invented the iPhone. That insight came from a keen and unique and special understanding about the company's users. In fact, even today, when you look at the Apple Store, they have applied the simplicity of their graphic user interface to the way in which people experience their retail environment. As a result, the Apple Store is one of the most profitable retailers in the world. They're responsible for knowing what their customers want, and they know they're not going to get there with surveys.

Surprisingly, I'm starting to see former executives from some of the worst corporations ever to exist in America, who are no longer with their companies, going out and teaching people how to deliver exquisite customer experience. We see failing hotel chains teaching customer experience programs, and amusement parks that have lost their way teaching courses on customer experience. It's insane! And unfortunately, many leaders, executives, and well-meaning companies don't honestly know where to turn. Because there's an agenda: Everything's going to be just fine. If you buy our software, if you buy our training package, if you let our consultants climb around your business for a few months, everything's going to be fine.

· · ·

"WHAT DO YOU HATE ABOUT ME?"

Customer experience is holistic. It begins with having an amazing work environment based on a culture of happiness. It's about really being honest with ourselves and asking ourselves some tough questions. And the toughest question is, "What do you hate about me?"

When was the last time you uttered those words? I mean, probably never. Because if you're like me, you do everything you can to make sure nobody would ever use such a strong word against you. But what I have found in looking at both the worst and the best organizations on the planet is that great organizations accept the fact that they're imperfect. They know that they do not serve a so-called customer, some monolithic archetype. They know they serve a wide range of personas. And they don't look at those personas from a perspective of demographics. They look at those personas from the perspective of what each person hates and loves. They also look at those hates and loves across the five touchpoints. And, of course, they look at them from the perspective of digital and physical environments. It's really hard to ask the question "What do you hate about me?" but it is the most powerful thing you and your organization can do to rapidly scale exquisite customer experiences.

THE ETERNAL QUESTION: DO CUSTOMERS ALWAYS KNOW WHAT THEY WANT?

In a perfect marketplace, the customer would always know exactly what they wanted, and the business would be able to provide it. The two—customer and business—would move in tandem, seamlessly, like Fred Astaire and Ginger Rogers doing a dance number in a Hollywood film. Each would keep step with the other, with no friction. Whatever the customer wanted, the customer got; and, to reduce waste to zero, the business would never produce anything the customer didn't want. The business would produce exactly what the market wanted—nothing less and nothing more.

That would be pretty good!

But then, to make the customer experience even better, imagine that the business knew what the customer wanted *before the customer did*. Wow! Imagine that!

The customer would say, "Gee, I want something . . . not sure what it is . . . something to make my life better . . . but I cannot describe it."

The business owner would reply, "Ah! I have exactly what you want. Here's the Gizmo 100! It's available right now!"

The delighted customer would exclaim, "OMG! The Gizmo 100 is exactly what I wanted but could not describe! Thank you!"

If such a system existed, it would be a win-win for both sides. The customer would be continually amazed and delighted, and the business could charge a premium price for its innovative products.

In fact, there are many businesses that try to do exactly that. Not only do they strive to produce what the customer wants, but they try to *anticipate* customer demand by producing goods that their customers either cannot articulate or would dismiss as being impossible.

The notion of the visionary leader who can conjure out of thin air products that people never knew they wanted until they saw them is attractive and powerful. It's also really *easy*! Why sweat over market research when you have a crystal ball?

Reality is far more nuanced. And contrary to popular mythology, two of the most famous innovators in history probably never meant what has been attributed to them.

Henry Ford's Faster Horse

The pioneering automaker Henry Ford has been quoted as saying, "If I had asked my customers what they wanted, they would have said a faster horse." The implication is that Ford saw a problem that no one else did, and invented a solution that no one anticipated.

First of all, there's no evidence he ever said this. Researchers have tried to find it, but in fact the first reference to it is from a 1999 article in the *Cruise Industry News Quarterly*, in which John McNeece, a designer of cruise ships, is quoted as saying, "There is a problem trying to figure out what people want by canvassing them. I mean, if Henry Ford canvassed people on whether or not he should build a motor car, they'd probably tell him what they really wanted was a faster horse."[1]

In fact, when Ford began building cars in the early 1900s, building a "faster horse" was never the issue. Horses were plenty fast. The problem—which Ford and many other car builders were acutely aware of—was that horses were incredibly inefficient. Even while not being used—that is, not producing value—you had to feed them and care for them. As Ford himself said in a 1923 interview with the *Christian Science Monitor*:

One man with a machine which perhaps he himself has helped to build, will do in a day as much as five men now do with their teams of horses. Horses on a farm are wasteful. Why, there are lots of small farms that have four and five teams of horses that stand idle three quarters of the time eating their heads off. In a few years the horse will become obsolete except for saddle horses, though why anyone wants to ride horse back is more than I can understand.[2]

Consumers at the turn of the twentieth century felt the pain of their horse-based transportation system. Manure piled high on city streets, turning to stinking mush by gallons of horse urine. Dead horses—by the tens of thousands—had to be dragged off to the glue factories. With the human population growing, the widespread use of horses for everyday labor and transportation was unsustainable. Everyone knew it, and everyone knew the automobile was the answer. The amazing thing about your automobile was that when it was not producing value—that is, when you weren't driving it—it could just sit there in your garage. It required no feeding, no care. It produced no manure. You could ignore it for days and even weeks, and that "downtime" cost you not one penny. When it stopped functioning, it did not turn into a fetid carcass.

The peak of the horse and mule population in the United States was 26.5 million in 1915. The human population was about 100 million. That made the ratio of horses to humans about 1:4. Imagine if that ratio continued unchanged. If it did, today we'd have 328 million people living with about 82 million horses. Instead, we have 276 million registered motor vehicles.

Let's look at another apocryphal quote—actually, three of them.

Steve Jobs and Customer Research

We are fortunate to have three authentic quotes from Steve Jobs, referenced in the biography by Walter Isaacson. These three quotes have been used—I think inappropriately—by people who assert that Jobs was a visionary who relied only on his own instincts, and that this is what everyone should do:

- At a 1982 planning retreat, a member of the Mac team suggested they do some market research to see what customers wanted. "'No,' [Jobs] replied, 'because customers don't know what they want until we've shown them.'"

- On the day he introduced the Macintosh, a reporter from *Popular Science* asked Jobs what market research he had done. Jobs replied, "Did Alexander Graham Bell do any market research before he invented the phone?"

- Jobs said, "Some people say, 'Give customers what they want.' But that's not my approach. Our job is to figure out what they're going to want before they do. I think Henry Ford once said, 'If I'd asked customers what they wanted, they would have told me, "A faster horse!"'" People don't know what they want until you show it to them. That's why I never rely on market research. Our task is to read things that are not yet on the page."[3]

These quotes, and others, are constantly touted as being evidence that Apple doesn't do market research. That would be big news to the Apple human resources department. As I was writing this, I went online and found this job opening advertised by Apple:

Apple's WW Product Marketing team is looking for an inspiring leader in Market Research to support its product research in key geographies. We're looking for someone who understands innovative research methodologies, analytics, and has extensive experience with translating data into impactful insights and linking it to business issues.[4]

I poked around some more, and decided to query the Apple "Jobs at Apple" database for "marketing analyst." My query returned 579 results. The query "stores market research analyst" provided six-hundred-plus results. And "iPhone Market Re-search & Analysis Manager" yielded this result, for a position at the headquarters in Cupertino. The description read in part, "This position is responsible for conducting qualitative and quantitative research to understand Apple's customers and de-veloping insights to support business decisions."[5]

Oh, and the *Wall Street Journal* did some digging into a patent dispute between Apple and Samsung, and among the court fil-ings, reporter Jessica E. Vascellaro found a golden nugget on the topic of "iPhone Owner Study" titled "Apple Market Research & Analysis, May 2011." It surveyed users in multiple countries about why they bought an iPhone.[6]

Let's get one thing settled: Apple uses very sophisticated mar-ket research.

So what's the answer? Market research or brilliant gut instinct? The answer is *both*.

Customer experience innovators like Henry Ford, Steve Jobs, Elon Musk, Jeff Bezos, and many others do not have some magi-cal power to see into the hearts and minds of consumers. They have the same market information you and I have. They feel the same pain points you and I feel.

- Henry Ford saw the pain caused by our centuries-old horse-based transportation system.

- Steve Jobs saw the pain caused by big, clunky, expensive computers.

- Elon Musk saw the pain caused by internal combustion vehicles. (The same ones that a century earlier had been so amazing when Henry Ford figured out how to mass-produce them.)

- Jeff Bezos saw the pain caused by inefficient brick-and-mortar retailers.

So what? Lots of people have had the same realizations. In the 1970s, many people thought, "Computers are cool, but why can't they be made simpler and easy to use?" As for electric cars, people have long tried to make them practical. (GM even had one in the late 1990s—the EV1, which they scrapped!) And even though retail stores could be fun places to visit, lots of people put up with them because they could not imagine a better alternative.

Every age has its innovators. The pain that Jeff Bezos saw was exactly the same pain that Richard Sears saw in 1893 when he launched the first Sears, Roebuck & Co. mail-order catalogue, whose success was made possible by the US mail system and the railroads. The early Sears catalogs were touted as the "Cheapest Supply House on Earth" or "the Book of Bargains," and featured a breathtaking range of products including musical instruments, medical and veterinary supplies, sewing machines, firearms, bicycles, and baby buggies. By 1894, the catalog had swelled to 322 pages. Richard Sears, who wrote most of the catalog's copy himself until his retirement in 1908, held to the motto "We can't afford to lose a customer," reflecting the company's relentless focus on eliminating hatepoints and garnering lovepoints.

"We can't afford to lose a customer"—not a bad slogan for any business!

If the pain these innovators saw was apparent to many, then why did they succeed?

They each had two important character traits:

1. They could imagine a solution.

2. They had the personal determination to make that solution a reality. As Thomas Edison said, "Genius is 1 percent inspiration, 99 percent perspiration." Therefore, character trait #1—imagining the solution—accounts for 1 percent of success. And character trait #2—personal determination to make that solution a reality—accounts for the other 99 percent.

That sounds about right!

TAKE ACTION!

Contrary to popular mythology, all successful entrepreneurs, whether selling to consumers or in the B2B space, have a keen grasp of what their customers want and don't want. They don't get this priceless information by intuition alone. There is no "secret shortcut" to knowing what your customers love and hate. It takes hard work and a willingness to hear difficult truths about what your customers want that may contradict your personal opinion.

Having said that, it's very possible that if you, as a consumer, hate something, it's likely that millions of other people hate it, too. This is the key to invention. It's all about seeing a problem in the marketplace and having what it takes to solve it: technology, willpower, and funding. Look at your organization and the market and ask yourself: "Where can we remove friction and make the customer experience as positive as possible?"

CHAPTER 8

TOUGH CHOICES
IN THE REAL WORLD

We understand that perfection may be an ideal, but it will never be attained. Not because we're dumb or lazy, but because the world itself is constantly changing, and in an entity as complex as a business, even a small one, it's simply impossible to make every aspect and operation of the company reach perfection.

There's another reason. It's because running a business is a balancing act. When you increase one area, another must decrease—and hatepoints sneak in. Here's an example. There's an old saying that every service business is concerned with price, speed, and quality. You can have two out of three, but never all three. If you want speed and quality, then price goes up. If you want a low price and good quality, then speed must go down. And if you want a low price and high speed, then quality must suffer. You can never have high quality, high speed, and low price. It's just not going to happen.

To that list of three we must add one more: ethical. Customers are increasingly concerned not just about buying the product they want, but also about the culture of the company that produced it. Sure, you may produce the finest sneakers at a low price and deliver them quickly, but if in accomplishing this goal your customers learn that you're producing your sneakers in sweatshops, the hatepoints will pile up.

This means that no matter which combination you choose to pursue, you will rack up the lovepoints with customers who happen to agree with your choices, and you will be bombarded with hatepoints from those who want what you're not giving them.

There are examples of this everywhere. For example, airlines are a service industry. They provide transportation from Airport A to Airport B using a mix of quality, speed, and price. In this case, by quality we mean the creature comforts enjoyed by the passengers, since in every other regard the quality of one flight or another is the same—you get where you're going.

THE SOUTHWEST AIRLINES "CATTLE CALL"

Southwest Airlines was founded in 1971 as a low-cost carrier. That meant their goal was to get the customer from Airport A to Airport B at the lowest cost and with the greatest convenience while still meeting every safety standard. The focus was on speed and price. Quality—meaning the extras that many airlines provided—was a distant third.

One of the hallmarks of the airline was the elimination of assigned seats. Instead, passengers received only a section assignment—A, B, or C. When your section was called to board the plane, you could take any open seat in your section. Analysis showed that this method allowed the plane to board quickly, saving time at the gate; and in the airline business, time is money.

This lasted until 2007, when the airline concluded that the system had introduced an *inefficiency*—namely, passengers were arriving at the gate early, in order to claim a spot in line. To save their passengers the stress of thinking they had to arrive early, Southwest modified its boarding procedure by introducing a number. Each passenger received the usual letter (A, B, or C), but also a number 1 through 60. When the plane boarded, the passengers lined up in numerical order within each letter group and, as usual, chose any open seat on the aircraft. According to a 2012 study by *Mythbusters*, this is the fastest method currently in use for non–first class passengers to board a plane. On average, it is ten minutes faster than the standard method used by most airlines of boarding from the back frontward.[1]

Passengers who aren't used to this system, or just hate it, have long called it the "cattle call." Southwest has always received hatepoints on their boarding approach, and yet has decided that courting more lovepoints by adopting assigned seats would raise costs and eventually cause many customers to defect. The core value proposition is affordable travel, and that's the brand identity.

Southwest makes it easy on passengers in other ways. While most US airlines charge passengers for checked luggage, Southwest continues to permit two free checked bags per passenger. And for those last-minute itinerary changes, Southwest also does not charge any change fees; passengers are permitted to change their flight as late as ten minutes prior to boarding.

It may be surprising, but according to Statista, Southwest ranks near the bottom in the number of customer complaints (being at the bottom is good).[2] Southwest Airlines has consistently received the fewest ratio of complaints per passenger boarded of all major US carriers that have been reporting statistics to the Department of Transportation (DOT) since 1987, which is when the DOT began tracking customer satisfaction statistics and publishing its Air Travel Consumer Report.

Why is this? Because Southwest is *transparent*. They deliver what they promise. Their customers—134.1 million in 2019—know what to expect. They understand the trade-off, and accept it.

Given the inevitability of getting some hatepoints for a choice you've made for your business, you're better off by being honest and telling your customers exactly what to expect. After all, you can't hate what you willingly accepted after being fully informed. Consumers may hate many things, including the cattle call at the boarding gate, but what they hate most of all is being deceived.

THE INFAMOUS IKEA INSTRUCTION SHEETS

The Swedish multinational conglomerate IKEA is known globally for its ready-to-assemble furniture, kitchen appliances, and home accessories. Founded in Sweden in 1943, since 2008 IKEA has been the world's largest furniture retailer. The company is known for its relentless attention to cost control, which has allowed it to maintain rock-bottom prices for its furniture. If you know a college student or young person living in their first apartment or starter house, it's almost a certainty you'll find it furnished with IKEA products.

To keep manufacturing and shipping costs down, IKEA sells most of its furniture in pieces, which the customer must assemble at home. This strategy of extreme "knock-down"—the industry term for disassembly of products to make them easier and cheaper to ship to customers—is a big reason why IKEA furniture is so affordable.

So that you, the customer, can assemble your item, each comes packed with a set of instructions, as well as the simple tools(s) required to do the job. Because IKEA is a global company, to save in printing costs, they design their instruction sheets using only pictures, no words. That way, a customer in Nepal can use the same set of instructions as one in the United States.

Obviously, this reliance on customer labor drives down the quality of the customer experience, especially when you consider that many competing furniture retailers advertise free delivery and setup of equivalent items. And the IKEA instruction sheets have achieved a near-mythological status, something that has been acknowledged by the company.

"A newspaper in Sweden described Ikea [furniture assembly] as something between civil engineering and captaining a submarine, and I think that's a good description," Allan Dickner, IKEA's deputy packaging manager, told *Fast Company*.[3]

IKEA also benefits from the fact that other retailers that make you assemble their products have instructions that are far more confusing than IKEA's, which are very carefully crafted. To paraphrase Winston Churchill's famous line, IKEA may be the worst form of ready-to-assemble product design we have—except for all the others.

Perhaps in recognition of the hatepoints its customers were heaping on IKEA because of assembly frustration, in 2017 the retailer acquired the gig-economy service company TaskRabbit for an undisclosed sum. At that time, around sixty thousand "taskers" used the platform to connect with people who needed odd jobs done, such as deliveries, household tasks—and constructing IKEA furniture.

"In a fast-changing retail environment," said Jesper Brodin, chief executive of IKEA, to the *New York Times*, "we continuously strive to develop new and improved products and services to make our customers' lives a little bit easier. Entering the on-demand, sharing economy enables us to support that."[4]

Sure enough, in 2018, IKEA announced TaskRabbit services would be available to customers at two West Coast stores. *Business Insider* reported that, after checkout, customers at the Emeryville and East Palo Alto, California, IKEA stores could book a tasker to assemble the furniture when they got home. Customers would be able to select the IKEA products they have bought from a list and get a quote on how much they cost to assemble.[5]

This is an approach we see over and over again with nimble, innovative companies. They create a solid business strategy in which they focus on key attributes—in the case of IKEA, it's been stylish furniture at rock-bottom prices. But there are pain points for the customer—again, for IKEA, it's been the self-assembly. (Actually there are more pain points associated with how the vast stores are designed to funnel you through a seemingly endless maze that forces you to visit each department . . . but that would be another chapter!) To IKEA's credit, they correctly identified this source of hate, but they also correctly decided that offloading product assembly onto the customer was an indispensable part of their product marketing. They could not afford to do away with the "flat pack" and the wordless instructions and take on the additional expense of assembling and shipping millions of pieces of furniture every year. So they made it easy for their customers to pay extra for assembly. This eased a chronic source of hatepoints and kept the balance in favor of lovepoints. And that's the name of the game: increase the lovepoints while decreasing the hatepoints.

FACEBOOK ALLOWS HATE . . .
AND IS HATED FOR IT

Facebook is the world's largest and most influential social media platform. By the beginning of 2021, the internet juggernaut, founded in 2004 by Mark Zuckerberg and his college friends, had grown to boast 2.8 billion monthly active users in nearly every industrialized nation on earth. Out of all the social media platforms, Facebook has the highest number of active users, and many people spend hours a day scrolling through their Facebook feeds. For them, Facebook isn't just a social media platform, it's a way of life.

Facebook has long insisted that it is not a publisher but rather a tech company that more closely resembles an uncontrolled community bulletin board where you can post just about anything (except nudity, which is easy to identify and remove). It has long resisted entreaties to more closely police the content its users post. It was clear from the beginning that Zuckerberg valued growth above all other considerations, and to appear to choose which voices were heard on the platform would slow down its phenomenal growth curve.

As the platform attracted the attention of extremists who realized its power to reach people directly, with no filter, Facebook evolved from a space where you could socialize with family and friends into a battleground of ideas and even propaganda.

The problem is that on social media, what one person loves, another will hate. This stands in contrast to the average product brand in the marketplace, which can easily identify what the majority of its customers love and hate. At McDonald's, people love hot, crispy French fries, and they hate cold, soggy ones. They love prompt, courteous service, and they hate rude, surly cashiers. These problems should be easy to identify and fix.

Social media, in which the "product" is generated by the users themselves, has no standards of quality. Even the distinction between "lies" and "truth" can be hard to draw. It's easy to identify threats; if you post "I want to kill so-and-so" on Facebook, the company will delete it and the police will come knocking on your door. This would be an easy call for the company to make. But opinions are subjective, especially when applied to public figures. You can say that an elected official is the worst excuse for a human being, might be a criminal, might be a Chinese spy, might be this or that . . . And it's acceptable free speech. But it's guaranteed to elicit hatepoints from Facebook users who happen to love that particular public figure. And their hate won't be directed only at the person—real or fraudulent—who made the post; it will be directed at the company itself for allowing such speech to remain.

"Companies like Facebook have a tough time navigating hate speech," said Ryan Calo, legal fellow at Stanford Law School's Center for Internet & Society, to NBC News in 2010. "Not only do they have to pick winners in content, they have to do it on a global scale. If they take down content because it offends one group of people, they end up offending another group."[6]

Many of Facebook's most loyal users have intense feelings of both love and hate for the company. Here's what an anonymous teen posted on the website Teen Ink in 2011:

I hate Facebook. That's a lie; I hate that I love Facebook. I, along with 500 million other active Facebook users, have an obsession. . . . It is an addiction. Facebook is like a cult; its empire keeps growing and growing, sucking in thousands of new helpless users each day, gaining more and more information about its victims, inevitably hooking each and consuming their lives. Yet we don't seem to have a problem with this.[7]

As the years passed, various world leaders began using the platform as a way to communicate directly with their audiences. Sometimes they did this by engaging in what Facebook's own Implementation Standards would call hate speech. Analysts became increasingly convinced that Facebook was putting immense effort into appearing to control its product, but only to mollify critics who were piling on the hatepoints. Mark Zuckerberg's vague decisions about abusive world leaders made sense when viewed as an outgrowth of his business model. "The company's incentive is to keep people on the platform," wrote Andrew Marantz in the *New Yorker* in October 2020, "including strongmen and their most avid followers, whose incendiary rhetoric tends to generate a disproportionate amount of engagement."[8] For Facebook, revenues come from ads and other content that have a high level of engagement, which is exactly what provocative content generates.

Facebook survives—and thrives—because users are willing to put up with what they hate about it in order to enjoy its benefits. As Christianna Silva wrote for Mashable in March 2021, "For a lot of users, it isn't that they don't want to delete their Facebook accounts—it's that Facebook has become so intertwined with the way they live online that they can't really escape it. To leave Facebook would be to shift the way they interact with the internet. . . . Whether we want it to be or not, Facebook is now a part of our internet DNA."[9]

Like many businesses that depend on a growing base of customers, Facebook has made the calculation that while it can—and should—police content that is obviously offensive to anyone, it would rather absorb the hatepoints from some users and stakeholders, including members of the US Congress who have been highly critical of the company, as a trade-off for the advertising dollars from those who love how they can benefit from the platform.

THE HATE SAFARI

In order to manage the level and intensity of the customer hate directed at your company or brand, you need to carefully gather it, understand it, and then work to reduce it. The first two steps—gathering and understanding—cannot be passive. Your company must proactively seek feedback from customers. Their opinions will not be handed to you on a silver platter, especially if you're a CEO or manager without direct customer contact. You need to cultivate them and value each complaint or bad review as an opportunity to do better.

The best organizations conduct regular "hate safaris" across their key touchpoints to seek out and observe firsthand how the customer is engaging their organization.

While the name may be humorous, the intent is serious. Go to the websites or physical stores of your competitors. Keep your eyes and ears open. Be a normal shopper. Make a small purchase. Notice all the customer touchpoints, and how they make you feel.

In your restaurant, you should be looking through the eyes of your customer. What does your entranceway look like? We worked with a restaurant chain that routinely had disgustingly dirty doors, which communicated the story to the customer of uncleanliness.

What does your business smell like, feel like, look like? What is the net totality of the experience at this very important touchpoint?

UNDERCOVER BOSS:
THE CEO EXPERIENCES LIFE IN THE TRENCHES

One of my favorite TV shows is *Undercover Boss*. This reality show has a simple premise: The CEO or top executive of a big company is sent to one of his or her company's locations as a lowly, entry-level employee. To avoid recognition, the CEO is outfitted with a disguise—wig, eyeglasses, tattoos, and so on. During the hour-long show, the CEO—who may lack the job skills required for his temporary position—works shoulder-to-shoulder with other employees and serves customers. Both hatepoints and lovepoints are racked up. Invariably, the CEO is astounded to learn how little he or she knows about the daily labor of the employees and their interactions with customers.

A memorable episode featured Rick Silva, the CEO of Checkers and Rally's, one of the nation's largest chains of double drive-thru restaurants. In his first assignment working in a restaurant in Homestead, Florida (each show typically has four assignments), Silva was appalled by the abusive manner with which the general manager treated his employees. Silva worked at the fry station of the restaurant alongside an employee named Todd, who dreamed of being a chef. The manager, a man named Stevens, sharply told Todd to shut up and work faster. At one point, Stevens threatened to take Todd outside and beat him for not working hard enough.

When Silva asked Todd why he allowed himself to be treated so badly, Todd replied that he had to keep his job so he could support his mother, and he worried that if he stood up for himself, he would be fired.

Silva was so upset that he took Stevens outside, and after an unsatisfactory discussion, revealed his true identity. After telling the shocked Stevens to go home, he closed the restaurant for the night. The next day it reopened with a new general manager, and Stevens was sent for more training.

Silva took responsibility for the manager's poor behavior, saying it was his own fault as CEO that the company didn't have the proper training procedures in place. And as for Todd, Silva awarded him with $15,000 to take care of his mother and additional money to finish culinary school.

Find the hatepoints and fix them, and your business will flourish!

TAKE ACTION!

While perfection may be an ideal, it will never be attained. You cannot reach it in all four key areas of low price, fast service, best quality, and high ethics. To attain one, another must decline, and the hatepoints will accumulate.

Consequently, running a business is a balancing act. As a decision maker, you must prioritize what you want your customers to love you for, and try to minimize what they will hate you for. Then you must craft your marketing effort to be in alignment with reality. Your customer will hate you less if you are up front about what you value and the negative aspects you expect your customer to tolerate.

CHAPTER 9

LESSONS FROM THE CUSTOMER EXPERIENCE HAZMAT TEAM

In my professional life working with global brands, I've often accepted the task of mopping up after failed customer experience initiatives. In doing this work, which I've dubbed "customer experience hazmat triage," I've learned what typically goes wrong in a very practical way.

But before I go on to discuss these disasters, I have a confession to make: I've made a lot of these same mistakes myself. As an advisor to some great companies, like many other professionals, there was a time when I accepted "customer experience best practices." But as I began to fix so many of these failed initiatives, I was able to see the true outcomes of these so-called best practices. These insights changed the way in which I helped my clients do a better job of leading their markets in customer experience.

Here are the key unmet challenges in the area of customer experience.

CUSTOMER EXPERIENCE DYSPHORIA

The word *dysphoria* means "a state of unease or generalized dissatisfaction with life." When used in the context of customer experience, it means that nagging feeling of lovepoints being spoiled by hatepoints. You wish your customer experience could be better, but it isn't, and you feel helpless to change it.

Why is customer experience producing dysphoria? It's primarily because organizations don't really know just how bad they really are. To put it more simply, they don't realize how many customers are not dedicated to them at best, and *hate* them at worse.

Too many businesses believe they're a lot better than they actually are.

Bain & Company recently did a survey of the customers and executives of 362 companies. Only 8 percent of the customers described their experience with the company with which they had interacted as "superior." Meanwhile, 80 percent of the executives surveyed at those same companies believed that the experience they had been providing to their customers was indeed superior.

That's an astonishing gap.

A similar study was done by Pegasystems, a leader in software for customer engagement and operational excellence. They asked leaders and employees to rate the quality of service their organization provided, from "terrible" to "excellent." Then they asked customers to rate the quality of a typical experience on the same scale.

The results?

- Forty percent of company *leaders* rated their company's service as "excellent."

- Twenty-three percent of company *employees* rated their company's service as "excellent."

- Ten percent of the company's *customers* rated the company's service as "excellent."

The gaps here, with more than two times the number of employees and four times the number of business leaders as customers deeming the quality of service as excellent, highlighted the fact that businesses in general are overconfident about the service they provide. The gap gets worse the further away you get from actually interacting with a customer. The frontline workers were mildly overconfident, while the executives, who probably had zero customer contact, were wildly overconfident.[1]

This points to another issue that I'll explore in the pages ahead: namely, the reluctance of many customers to express dissatisfaction directly to the company. Instead of speaking up, they shrug their shoulders and think, "Well, once again I got lousy service. What can you do?" But when asked by a third-party researcher, they're suddenly willing to go on the record and say, "Yes, the service provided by XYZ Company was terrible. I'm never shopping there again." Meanwhile, the executives at XYZ Company, while on their annual retreat to a resort in Jamaica, are blissfully unaware of how much their own customers hate them. They act like Alfred E. Neuman and repeat the mantra, "What, me worry?"

I suppose you could suggest that it's not surprising that executives and leaders and board members believe their organizations deliver far better customer experience than in reality. When you take a look at the way in which we glean insights about customer sentiment, we use surveys and promoter scores and just about any tool we possibly can, and too often they provide the prejudicial idea that we're good. Although it might make for really impressive charts and graphs and presentations, the information that we glean from these outdated programs is often irrelevant or completely erroneous; and, most importantly, it doesn't provide actionable insights on how to drive better experiences. We believe we're much better than we are.

THE CUSTOMER EXPERIENCE INDUSTRIAL MONSTER

The systems that make up the customer experience industrial monster have been designed to make companies and leaders look better than they actually are. That's the first thing we need to change. We need to change the way we get insights about what customers really care about, across a range of hate/love personas. Throughout the customer's journey, both digital and physical, customer experience is failing because the systems we use were created in a time that didn't have the level of hyper-competition that we do today. Today, as a result of what I've named the C-19 economy, consumers have been "hyper-consumerized." With just a few clicks, they're accustomed to getting something at their front door in just a few hours. Friction is a killer. But most organizations have baked friction into their organizational processes, and this is especially true in the way they deliver experiences to their customer.

The other reason that customer experience is failing is that we're currently in a time of hyper-competition. In the old days, we would just compete against another competitor. Today, new economic models and new value models are not just displacing our competitors, they're displacing the way in which value is distributed to the customer. That means that competition is literally coming from every compass direction. The differentiator in a time of hyper-competition and hyper-consumerization is the way in which we deliver experiences across the customer's journey.

PRINCIPAL FOCUS OF
CUSTOMER ACQUISITION OVER RETENTION

Another major cause of customer experience disaster is the fact that organizations try to make up for the loss of their existing customers from bad customer experiences. In fact, most organizations today are singularly obsessed with getting *new* customers. At some level, this makes perfect sense; after all, we're in the business of getting and serving customers. The problem is that they are so focused on getting more customers that they lose complete and total sight of *customer retention* and *customer promotion.* It's not uncommon to see ten times the budget dedicated to customer acquisition over customer retention and promotion. It's amazing that in a time of hyper-competition, we're spending our money exclusively on trying to find more customers while our current customers are leaving the building. This is not a small matter, because customer attrition is a huge problem for organizations, yet it is widely ignored. We're losing customers because we keep doing things they hate.

Customer experience is nothing more than an *innovation activity.* When we understand the systems and the superpower of innovation, we can certainly see how this new body of research can have an incredible impact in the way in which organizations enjoy and drive sustainable growth and profitability.

GET ACCURATE CUSTOMER INSIGHTS—
AND ACT ON THEM

Organizations love to use ubiquitous and outdated promotion scores and surveys because they are the safe choice and considered to be the best practice. No manager has ever gotten fired for using the same customer satisfaction tools that everyone else in his or her industry uses! The problem is that these systems do not provide actionable innovations that change the way in which consumers experience a company and its service. Promotion scores and surveys, along with other old-fashioned methods, can serve as data points, but nothing more.

The answer is to frontload the process of delivering exceptional customer services by improving the time and resources we invest in insights. One example of a method I use with tremendous success is customer experience hackathons.

Customer Experience Hackathons

In this activity, we take customer-facing stakeholders, and we go through an innovation and ideation activity, which gets them to help us build our personas of hate and love. Then we invent new experiences across the five touchpoints that are also blended. I've conducted hundreds of customer experience innovation hackathons, which have subsequently generated tens of millions of dollars in enterprise value. And guess what? The insights didn't come from a fancy consultant or lame survey. They came from employees who woke up every day and served the organization.

We can fix customer insights by having an intelligent and thoughtful balance of how we use promotion information, surveys, and all insights, as we need to aggregate these more thoughtfully. We absolutely need to add additional new ways to get far more interesting and actionable insights that can instantly be deployed as a new innovation, just as the best organizations are doing.

The worst organizations rely on "phoning it in" with a survey or some other out-of-the-box software solution. Customer experience insights is not a technology stack, software solution, or any other machine. Those can be useful, of course, but if we rely on those without the human connection piece, we're really asking for trouble.

Appropriate CX Technologies

That brings me to the second problem that we often found during our hazmat triage. Enabling technologies, such as most customer experience (CX) technologies, when we really look at them, are either risk management tools, marketing tools, or reporting tools. Very few technology stacks or software solutions deliver the insights and the experience that allow us to master customer experience and lead our marketplace.

To be clear, I regularly suggest technologies to my clients. These technologies should always be used for good instead of evil. And by that I mean we need to use these technologies to get insights about what they *love* as well as insights about what our customers *hate*. We need to use technologies to increase our access to customers. We need to use our technologies to not just find ways to upsell, cross-sell, and market to them, but to improve their experience. In our research, we found many instances where organizations were talked into a bad technology purchase by some salesman. And, of course, predictably, it failed miserably.

Collaboration Is King

In our hazmat activity, we nearly always found a problem with collaboration with both team members and the customer alike. This is a big problem because some of these organizations seem to be actually *hiding* from their customers. It was incredible just how little they really knew about their customers' experiences across the five touchpoints.

For example, we worked with an automotive dealership that didn't realize how much their customers hated their service department. The people in sales were working very hard to deliver great experiences. But they had eight people in their service department who despised their customers! All the money they spent trying to get people in the door and trying to address customer experience in the front end was quickly destroyed at the first oil change.

Customer experience must be exceptional at *all five touchpoints*—and that requires collaboration among the various departments and team members who will, at some time, all interact with the same customer.

We once worked with a large organization that manufactured equipment for restaurants. Their marketing team, salespeople, and CEO were incredible. Unfortunately, the warranty department was a disaster. Too often a loyal customer would send a piece of equipment to be repaired under warranty and have a terrible experience. The previously happy customer would immediately loathe the entire company. There was really no way for the salespeople to know that because they didn't have the insights to find out why customers were leaving.

Collaboration is imperative across departments that touch the customer, so that you can architect an innovation strategy across all touchpoints.

Another big hazmat discovery was the lack of customer experience training, and in some cases the absolute wrong training. Now, there are two ways to look at stakeholder training around customer experience and customer service. There's one group of companies that we found had hired training companies to come in and basically train the employees to stop being so mean to their customers!

THE POWER OF TIERED TRAINING

It's hard to imagine that leaders in major organizations are naïve enough to assume that the only thing they need to do to fix customer experience is to train their customer-facing stakeholders to provide what their customers like. If you're looking to really rule the day when it comes to customer experience and customer experience innovation, there is absolutely no question that training is mandatory. But it's not the only thing you have to do. If you don't fix the things that customers *hate*, all of the training in the world is not going to resolve anything. Too many organizations deliver customer service training that is not job specific, and it's typically not relevant to an organization's culture and industry. Our research proves that the best way to build a core competency of customer experience in an organization is to break it up into three tiers.

1. Customer Experience Master Training (Strategic Training)

Company culture begins at the top and filters its way down. The rise of the chief experience officer (CXO), an executive position overseeing CX strategy implementation, is bringing CX to the highest level of an organization's structure and goals. Many organizations need integral changes to their core systems to put the customer at the center, around which they can build memorable experiences. Each member of an organization needs to know how their role impacts the organization and, ultimately, the bottom line—and this must begin at the very top.

This level of training is for C-suite executives who ultimately determine the customer experience within their enterprise. It's designed to provide the skills necessary to build core competency in the area of customer experience innovation. This includes the impact of stakeholder happiness, innovation pipeline management, customer experience ideation, and overarching customer experience leadership skills.

The entire customer journey must be exceptional, because even if employees execute well on individual touchpoint interactions, the overall experience can still disappoint. The only people in the position to see the big picture are the top executives, and they must have both a clear vision and the will to make it a reality.

2. Customer Experience Advocacy Training (Manager Training)

This level of training is for managers of customer-facing stakeholders. The training is specifically designed to provide actionable insights on how to support customer experience champions. This training is extremely comprehensive because it addresses the global landscape of customer experience management. This course is a prerequisite for master training.

It takes patience and determination to train managers to see the world through the customer's eyes and to redesign functions to create value in a customer-centric way. The management task begins with considering the customer—not the organization—at the center of the exercise.

Disruptive technology and intense competition have given customers unprecedented power to demand the experiences they want when purchasing goods and services. Over 70 percent of them, research finds, expect problem-solving service within five minutes of making contact online. They want a simple experience, and expect from every business the same level of immediacy, personalization, and convenience that they receive from leading practitioners such as Amazon and Google.

3. Customer Experience Champion Training (Customer-Facing Training)

This extremely important training is targeted to address issues such as empathy, communication skills, engagement techniques, and conflict resolution. This training also creates the linkage between the stakeholder's quality of life and the way in which they deliver experiences to customers. This course is a prerequisite for advocacy training.

As you can see, it's incredibly important to train employees in a way that is highly relevant to how they engage the customer, as well as use the customer experience deployment and strategy.

An exquisite customer experience depends on a collective, organization-wide conviction and sense of purpose to serve the customer's true needs. This purpose must be communicated to every employee through a simple, powerful statement of intent: a shared vision and aspiration that's authentic and consistent with a company's brand-value proposition. For example, a widely recognized shared vision is the common purpose of the Walt Disney Company: "We create happiness by providing the finest in entertainment for people of all ages, everywhere."

As Disney teaches in its professional development training courses, the company's key to creating "magical guest interactions" stems from its common purpose. For example, at the theme parks (the business segment with the strongest focus on the customer experience), Disney cast members understand that their primary goal is to create happiness—what Disney calls "magical moments." From park greeters to attraction attendants to those in backstage support roles, every decision they make regarding a guest interaction is focused on "creating happiness."[2]

Training is key. When employees can see clearly how their particular role fits into the big picture, they are more able to not just meet, but exceed, customer expectation.

——————————TAKE ACTION!——————————

Your business comprises many moving parts—that is to say, various departments that are managed by people who have independent minds. In your mission to identify and reduce sources of customer hate, the first step is to uncover and recognize reality. But this alone is not sufficient. The next step is to ensure that every person who works for you is in alignment with the mission and values articulated by leadership. Here, *self-awareness* is key. Your people must know and understand organizational priorities, and be willing to strive for measurable results.

Training at all levels is key. Consider it not a cost but an investment in the future success of your organization.

CHAPTER 10

YOUR EMPLOYEES CREATE LOVEPOINTS

When trying to uncover the source of customer attrition, many organizations ask a simple question: "What's missing? Why are we not collecting truckloads of lovepoints from our customers?"

They realize their customer experience initiatives are not working. Their customers aren't any happier than they were prior to the development and deployment of what they thought was a comprehensive customer experience strategy. So what was missing? Of course, it's impossible to answer that question without an assessment of their specific initiative. But far too often, I see that the problem lies with the culture of the company itself. By this I mean that happiness is contagious. It spreads easily from person to person, and from employee to customer. The obverse is also true: employee misery is equally contagious. Sullen, disengaged employees create sullen, disengaged customers, who then take their business elsewhere.

Every organization—large or small, profit or nonprofit, B2B or B2C—must be able to look itself in the mirror and see what's real. They must see what their customer sees, without excuses or defensiveness.

To build an organization dedicated to the idea that happy employees create happy customers, it's a good idea to start with the basics and work from there.

POSITIVE CUSTOMER EXPERIENCE DEFINED

What is a positive customer experience (CX)? Here's a very simple definition:

> *Positive customer experience is the creation of novel value that serves your organization and your customers.*

That's it. That's what positive customer experience is. We know that if we can't define a CX innovation program in a way that creates actionable activities, and that moves the needle in terms of customer satisfaction and loyalty, then it's been a failure.

When we dissect the anatomical structure of the definition, we see that there are components that require a bit more definition.

In the first part of the definition, *novel* means "new." It doesn't have to be new to the universe, it just has to be new to your organization, or applied in a new way.

Value is the tricky part of the definition because it lives across a spectrum of meanings. It can be incremental, it can be landmark, it can be breakthrough, or it can be disruptive. The best organizations create customer experience innovations that live across a value portfolio. In other words, it's important to have *incremental innovations*. Applied over a period of time, they are a tremendous way to manage continuous process and continue experiential value. But as we go into those higher value areas, these are characterized by bigger breakthroughs and significant innovations. We need a combination of these various levels of value in order to have a diverse portfolio that is living across risk and reward.

FOCUS ON THE MISSION

The other component of the definition is your organization's mission. If an activity isn't serving your mission, it's probably not something that you should be doing. The good news is that if it serves your mission, it's probably going to serve the customer. In other words, if you can find new ways to be more effective and more efficient in the way in which you deliver experiences, you'll save money, and that savings can be passed along to your customer. These all work together, so once again we have to define customer experience for what it is: an innovation activity. My definition of customer experience is different from those who are struggling to make innovation and customer experience real.

Your employees deliver your company's mission to your customers. If your employees know the mission and believe in it, then they'll be more engaged and motivated to spread the good vibes to their customers. The difference will impact your bottom line. There have been numerous studies showing the correlation between positive culture and high performance, with one example showing that, since 1998, *Fortune*'s "100 Best Companies to Work For" (a good proxy for companies with a strong culture) have outperformed the S&P 500 by a factor of two to one.[1]

That's not bad!

Now let's look at the other things that are necessary.

A STRATEGY FOR BUILDING HAPPINESS

The other thing that is missing from most organizations, and the reason why they're not delivering exquisite experiences to their customers, is they don't have happiness as an enterprise strategy.

Happiness as an enterprise strategy is mandatory.

When I wrote my first book on customer experience, *What Customers Crave*, I was surprised to see the direct corollary between Yelp ratings provided by customers and Glassdoor ratings provided by employees. You can see for yourself that customer ratings track with those posted by employees. That fact shouldn't be lost on us. As I will repeat throughout this book, if we want to deliver happy *experiences*, we first need to create a happy *culture*.

In my continuing research, looking at thousands of companies, I see it over and over again. Oftentimes, it's a culture that begins with the CEO, or even the board of directors. In other words, the board of directors and the CEO are absolutely responsible for stakeholder happiness—and that includes employees, suppliers, and customers. Because if they don't support the stakeholder community, there's no way you'll have meaningful and scalable improvements in the way in which you deliver great experiences.

The other thing that's important to understand about happiness is that it's a product of a culture of inclusion. It's a culture of accepting the differences that are beautiful and that make our stakeholders and our customers special. If you don't have an honest conversation about inclusion, you'll never move toward a culture of happiness.

GIVING EMPLOYEES A VOICE

The overwhelming majority of stakeholders want to have a voice. They want to collaborate around the ideas and projects they're going to be responsible for deploying. They want to feel that they're doing far more than exchanging the days of their life for cash. They want to be involved in a mission that matters. They want their organization to be involved in the authorship of their personal evolution. And most importantly, they want to know that your organization cares about providing real and meaningful value to your customers.

Typically missing in most customer experience initiatives are these key concepts, the omission of which results in predictable failure:

- The company has no actionable definition of customer experience.

- Happiness is not even on their radar. The concept of having happiness as an enterprise strategy is almost arcane.

- Their customer experience and innovation activities are disparate and poorly deployed. They really don't have measurables inside about what their customers and their stakeholders care about.

- From the training perspective, they don't do job-specific training. And, as a result of that, the employees are confused and left to their own devices.

- They don't have a formal customer experience strategy that ensures they deploy a holistic solution with proper measurements. That includes all of the things necessary to make sure the entire customer experience ecosystem will work.

Do you like Top 10 lists? I do. I made a Top 10 list to share with you the things typically missing from most organizations when it comes to the successful, scalable, and profitable return of customer experience initiatives.

Here's my list of the ten worst causes of customer experience initiative failure—and the solutions.

THE TOP 10 CX KILLERS— AND THE SOLUTIONS

1. **No formal customer experience innovation strategy.** The employees who need to garner lovepoints from customers are often left in the dark to fend for themselves and offer their own personal interpretation of positive customer experience—which may not be positive at all! It's like the waitress who thinks it's charming to be rude to her customers. She thinks they'll love her because she's "got spunk." No, they don't love her—but they may never tell that to anyone except all their friends on social media.

   Solution: Formulate and implement a clear and measurable customer experience innovation strategy with stated goals, expected outcomes, and measurements. This must be company-wide and an integral part of the training of every customer-facing employee.

2. **Negative company culture incapable of delivering exquisite human experiences.** No CX strategy can succeed if the company culture is rotten. Too many companies adopt programs because they think they should or because a consultant told them they had to, and they fail because the employees think it's a joke or just something they should pretend to accept.

    Solution: Company culture always starts at the top. If you are the CEO, it's up to you to set the tone with clear company policies and effective training. You must personally model a positive company culture that puts the customer first. Your immediate subordinates—in a big company, your C-suite—will follow you. Their subordinates will follow them, and so on down to the people working the phones and cleaning the floors.

3. **Not sponsored and supported at the board and CEO level.** Too often, CX innovation programs are just that—"programs" that are adopted with great fanfare, branded with a catchy name, rolled out . . . and then left to wither due to lack of material support. Employees shrug and think it's just another slogan designed to "motivate" them.

    Solution: Having a positive company culture is good, and having a plan is necessary, but you must have material support to effect change. Put the CX innovation program in the annual budget. Give CX training a line item and assign someone to ensure it's viable across all departments of the company and during all four quarters of the year.

4. **No strategic training for CX leaders.** People working on the top floors of the office building often have little

firsthand experience in dealing with customers—or at least not since they had a summer job in their college days. For them, the problem can seem abstract, and not vividly real. This hampers their ability to speak with credibility on the issue.

Solution: You are never too old—or too high up the corporate food chain—to learn something new about how to make your organization stronger. Get training in the impact of stakeholder happiness, innovation pipeline management, customer experience ideation, and overarching customer experience leadership skills.

5. **No advocacy training for CX managers.** The managers are the key linchpins between corporate leaders and frontline staff, and if they aren't fully immersed in the CX innovation strategy, then it won't be effective.

Solution: Managers of customer-facing stakeholders need training specifically designed to provide actionable insights on how to support customer experience champions. This training needs to be comprehensive and address the global landscape of customer experience management, and in particular how to resolve problems and conflicts.

6. **No customer championship training for customer-facing employees.** No training means a higher number of negative interactions with customers and the accumulation of hatepoints with a deficit of lovepoints. If you're at McDonald's and your burger arrives cold and soggy, you don't blame CEO Chris Kempczinski. (You've probably never heard of him. He took over in 2015.) You don't blame the guy who owns the franchise restaurant. You blame the kid behind the counter who was goofing off while your

burger sat in its paper bag. Your unhappiness leads to lower sales and lost revenues. Yes, hatepoints cost money!

Solution: These employees are critically important because they directly interact with the customers and make sales. As they are judged by the customer, so is the company as a whole. The process of outstanding CX begins with hiring the right people. You can teach anyone to fry a burger for three minutes per side, but you cannot teach them to be happy. If you hire happy people, they train quickly and work better under pressure.

7. **The initiative is incomplete and poorly developed.** This is another example of a top executive having the idea that a CX innovation program would be good, but then dropping the ball when it's time for deployment and company-wide participation. As a result, the funds allocated are wasted and employees become cynical about yet another scheme from the head office designed to torment them.

    Solution: Ensure the initiative is more than just an "initiative." It needs to be a permanent part of the everyday operations of the company, with periodic reviews at the frontline, management, C-suite, and board levels.

8. **Based on outdated so-called "customer experience best practice."** Too many companies are living in the past. They haven't kept pace with the accelerating pace of customer experience innovation and the rapidly evolving ways in which their customers interact with the brand and bestow upon the company their lovepoints and hatepoints. This creates a disconnect with the marketplace, customer dysphoria, and eventual loss of revenue.

Solution: Listen to your customers—especially the younger ones, for whom a new technology is just business as usual. Listen also to your younger employees, who are likely to be in tune with emerging trends. Watch your customer demographics carefully. Beware of the "Oldsmobile effect," where you find your brand appealing to an increasingly older age group and fewer young people.

9. **No internal communication strategy on how stakeholders participate and benefit.** Companies often launch customer experience innovation programs with a big splash but then fail to "sell" it to every employee and stakeholder. People are often set in their ways, and view innovative programs with suspicion. They just don't want to get out of their comfort zones! As a result, because stakeholders don't see the benefit for them, the effort withers and dies.

Solution: Appoint a director who will be responsible for educating managers on how and why the CX innovation program will help them do their jobs and produce better outcomes. Create a forum or pipeline for feedback and success stories. Have that director report to the executive team, armed with data about customer retention and brand awareness on social media and other measurable platforms.

10. **Technology purchase disguised as a customer experience program.** It's a cop-out to just buy a chunk of software, a new phone tree system, or a customer tracking program, and expect the customer experience to get any better.

Solution: Even if your customer's experience is largely digital—as it is on Amazon.com—you still need human eyes on the data to interpret the story of customer interactions with your platform. Technology can be a useful tool only if its paired with human training and sustained human engagement.

The important thing to remember is that for every problem there is a solution! Many companies have suffered under the burden of hatepoints accumulated over years, only to come back strong and lean. A good example is General Motors, which at the time of its bankruptcy in 2009 represented everything you could hate about a company: bloated, arrogant, unresponsive to its customers, oblivious to innovation. But it came back, better than ever, and while it's no longer the number one carmaker—that honor goes to the Volkswagen Group, followed by Toyota, Daimler, Ford, and Honda—its cars are well respected and even innovative. In 2020, the venerable company unveiled its Ultium platform, a modular, highly flexible, third-generation global electric vehicle platform powered by proprietary Ultium batteries. The platform will allow the company to compete for nearly every customer in the market today, whether they are looking for affordable transportation, a luxury experience, work trucks, or a high-performance machine.

"Thousands of GM scientists, engineers, and designers are working to execute an historic reinvention of the company," said GM President Mark Reuss. "They are on the cusp of delivering a profitable EV business that can satisfy millions of customers."

It's hard to believe that just ten years earlier, GM was on the verge of being written off as a hopelessly arthritic dinosaur!

• • •

TAKE ACTION!

A positive customer experience is defined as "the creation of novel value that serves your organization and your customers."

The heart of the matter is that your employees cannot possibly create love from your customers if they themselves are full of hate for the company and their jobs. Happiness as an enterprise strategy is mandatory. If you want to deliver happy *experiences*, you first need to create a happy *culture*.

To attain this goal consistently, your organization must have a customer experience (CX) innovation program. Your CX innovation program must create actionable activities and move the needle in terms of customer satisfaction and loyalty.

CHAPTER 11

CUSTOMER EXPERIENCE INNOVATION

Something unsettling is happening out there in the world of commerce.

Every day, another organization realizes their competition is passing them by. And to make it even worse, new competitors are emerging with completely new value propositions that their customers absolutely love.

So what do these organizations do? In a time of massive, massive change, they retreat to the "best practice" playbook, and try to use what worked last year, or even ten years ago. While the marketplace is the subject of massive disruption, many organizations are doubling down on *sameness in a time of differentness*. And the results are devastating—at least for them. For their competitors, the results are very good!

To understand what's happening, we first need to understand *disruption*. A good definition is the following:

DISRUPTION =
RATE OF CHANGE X SIZE OF CHANGE

Change comes at different rates—slow or fast. It also comes at different amplitudes—small or large. (If this sounds like what you learned about electromagnetic energy in science class, you're right—the principles are the same.) You can increase either the rate or size of change, and thereby increase disruption. Or you can do what's been happening since the advent of the digital age: increase both rate *and* size.

Disruption sweeps across the marketplace in three key categories.

1. Customer Expectations

Ironically, as businesses get better at fulfilling customer expectations, their customers become accustomed to this "new normal," and soon want something more than what they're getting now.

If they can get delivery in three days, then that becomes normal. Soon they'll want two days, then one day.

If the jeans they buy come in a dozen sizes, soon they'll want jeans that are custom-fit.

If they can buy bananas in the dead of winter, soon they'll want fresh raspberries and strawberries, too.

If their smartphone can be used as a video camera, then soon they'll want the images to be high-definition feature film quality.

Just like everything else, *the rate of rising expectations* is rising. It's been rising ever since the dawn of the Industrial Revolution, and the innovations are coming at consumers faster than ever.

Product life cycles are getting shorter. The traditional cycle of introduction, growth, maturity, and decline is happening more quickly. The failure rate is high, too. According to a 2015 Nielsen survey of CPGs, the vast majority of new product introductions are taken out of distribution before the end of their launch year. The survey found that over a period of several years, sixty thousand new SKUs were introduced to the marketplace in Europe. Of those, only 55 percent made it to twenty-six weeks, and only 24 percent remained after one year.[1]

Across a range of industries, 50 percent of annual company revenues are derived from new products launched within the past three years. This suggests that long-term product "cash cows," which used to stay in a company's portfolio for many years, and even decades, are becoming increasingly rare. Brands must effectively adjust their supply chain, including their packaging, to align with ever-shrinking product life expectancy. Replacing a product or service line every two years is becoming the norm. And if a business is not quick to introduce a new product to market, it risks launching a product that has already been superseded by competitors.

2. Disruptive Technologies

The force that makes rapid change possible is technological innovation. Everyone senses this instinctively—and the data proves it.

The most famous proof of accelerating technology is Moore's Law. In 1965, Gordon Moore, the cofounder of Fairchild Semiconductor and Intel (and former CEO of the latter), posited that with improving manufacturing techniques, every year the number of components per integrated circuit would be doubled. He projected this rate of growth would continue for at least another decade. In 1975, looking forward to the next decade, he revised the forecast to doubling every two years, a compound annual growth rate (CAGR) of 41 percent. His prediction held, and has since become known as a "law."

This is not just an abstract piece of data. More powerful computers means more work can be done in a shorter amount of time. An acceleration in the rate of semiconductor progress contributed to a surge in US productivity growth, which according to the Federal Reserve Bank reached 3.4 percent per year in 1997–2004, outpacing the 1.6 percent per year during both 1972–1996 and 2005–2013.[2]

There are similar corollaries. For example, Gerald Butters, the former head of Lucent's Optical Networking Group at Bell Labs, proposed Butters' Law of Photonics, a formulation that says the amount of data that can be transmitted by an optical fiber is doubling every nine months. Thus, the cost of transmitting a bit over an optical network decreases by half every nine months.[3]

There is a downside to accelerating technological change. For consumers, while it means the reaping of lovepoints for cool new gadgets, it also means an equal and opposite production of hatepoints as those gadgets become obsolete. Consumers who loved their digital device when they bought it become enraged when the company, just a few years later, stops supporting their device, which means that it won't accept new apps and, if it breaks, the company won't fix it. According to the most recent estimate by the Environmental Protection Agency, Americans throw away 350,000 smartphones every day—that's over 127 million every year. Despite devices having a usable life span of about seven years, most people only use their phone for about eighteen months. And because of the toxic materials and deep resource footprint used in the production of many digital devices, obsolescence leads to significant negative environmental consequences.[4]

3. New Business Models

As customer expectations change and they demand more choices while technology advances, the two forces can converge to create not just new products and services but entirely new business models.

New business models emerge when a founder is sensitive to a customer hatepoint—spoken or unspoken—and decides to change it, and either purposefully or inadvertently invents an entirely new way of solving the problem.

We've seen this repeatedly throughout history, but more often in today's rapidly evolving marketplace. For example, in 2007, roommates Joe Gebbia and Brian Chesky couldn't afford their San Francisco rent. They knew a big design conference was coming to town, and hotel space was booking up quickly. Gebbia sent Chesky an email with an idea: What if they turned their vacant loft space into a simple bed-and-breakfast, with a sleeping mat and breakfast? It was a way to "make a few bucks." They bought three air mattresses and created a simple website, airbedandbreakfast.com. Their first guests, two men and one woman, showed up. Each guest paid $80 to sleep on an air mattress.

They recruited a third partner and kept tinkering with the idea. By the summer of 2008, the founders had designed the touchpoint journey so that it took only three clicks to book a stay. But venture capital investors had nothing but hate for the upstart company. Finally, in April 2009, Airbnb picked up a $600,000 seed investment from Sequoia Capital. The next year, Chesky famously lived exclusively in Airbnbs for a few months when their employees crowded out the bedroom space left in their apartment. He knew exactly the lovepoints and hatepoints experienced by their customers. By 2011—four years after those first three guests—Airbnb was in eighty-nine countries and had hit one million nights booked on the platform.[5]

Of course, with growth came new challenges and government regulation. But the floodgates were open, and a vast reservoir of hatepoints that travelers had against traditional hotels—chiefly the high price tags and impersonal service—was unleashed in favor of the new concept.

Other new, disruptive business models we've seen emerge in the twenty-first century include the "crowd economy" models of Uber and Lyft; the "free data" model of Google, Facebook, and Twitter; artificial intelligence, such as the driverless grocery delivery service Nuro; and decentralized autonomous organizations, which may run entirely without human management supervision.

Do customers love these new businesses? Yes!

Will they become accustomed to them, and want more? Yes!

Will the hatepoints pile up? They already are! With every problem solved, you introduce new problems and new possibilities for hate. You always must keep one step ahead. As you eliminate one hatepoint, keep your eyes peeled for the next one to spring up.

LAYERED AND DYNAMIC VALUE

Customer expectations, disruptive technologies, and new business models are the three dimensions of massive disruption. The baseline level of current customer expectation is rising rapidly. We also see the continuous impact of disruptive technologies and are challenged to see how we can leverage them in a thoughtful way to improve how we eliminate friction and become more relevant to our customers. Lastly, and certainly not least, great innovators disrupt their marketplace by creating new business models to deliver value to customers.

But let's go back to customer experience. If we are in a time of disruption—I think there's little argument that we aren't—then why are too many organizations not responding by significantly improving the way in which they deliver value to their customers? Why are they not striving to reduce hatepoints while boosting lovepoints? Sadly, too many organizations aren't approaching it this way.

Remember, disruption is the rate and size of change. That means we need to speed up, and we need to continuously create more value for our customers. There are many dimensions of that.

We need to create better products, better packaging, better ways to deliver.

To access technology, we need to take a look at the features and benefits of our products and services to make certain they're optimized.

Remember, customers want *layered and dynamic value*. Simply put, layered value means you're going to give them more than they expected. Dynamic value means the value that you deliver is constantly getting better. This is something that too many organizations fail at.

The creation of that value takes me to my next point. If we're going to add layered value, that means we have to create something that's *new*. If we're going to create dynamic value, that means we need to create something that's *new*.

What is the business process that we use to create newness? Drum roll, please. . . . Here it is: *Innovation* is the tool that creates newness.

It's important to note here that newness alone isn't valuable. For example, less than 2 percent of the three thousand or so patents filed each week in the US Patent and Trademark Office ever go on to be successfully commercialized. And that's why we want to use an innovation pipeline approach so we can evaluate the viability, the value, and all the things we need to look at to control the risk when we build new things. While innovation carries some risk of loss of investment, not innovating in a time of massive disruption, where the market and the customer are demanding more, is *far more risky*.

Another important point is that customer experience is super-serious. In a time of massive disruption, we must not use customer experience as a slogan or a bumper sticker. It must be functional within our organization, or we will fail, guaranteed. During many of my customer experience hazmat cleanups, we found that organizations were using CX to check a box. In other words, there was a board meeting, and during the board meeting there was a discussion that most customers were unhappy with the company, or even a few customers were unhappy with the company. And as a result of that, the board and administrative staff said, "Okay, we need to do something about it. Let's put in a customer experience strategy." They brought in XYZ Consulting, who talked to all the smart people in the organization. They cataloged the insights from those smart people who worked in the organization and then put it in a three-ring binder as if it were their own information.

Today, that three-ring binder is stashed in the deepest recesses of a file cabinet in the office of a manager, never again to be seen by human eyes.

That's really how it works out most of the time. You get a "cash-ectomy" from a consulting firm, and in return they give you a three-ring binder of the great insights that they got from your stakeholders.

We don't get to do that anymore. Today, we actually have to make this stuff real, and we have to actually do it. But if we do it from the perspective of "best practices," as most consulting firms do, we're in trouble. Because remember, we are in a disruptive market. Disruption is the rate and size of change. So we have to avoid the pitfalls of looking at customer experience from the perspective of a rearview mirror approach.

I know I've stressed this point. But it's interesting to me that I'll have these discussions with clients, and yet sometimes they're not willing to emotionally let loose of the warm, comfortable feeling of doing what they have done forever, no matter how disastrous the results.

Here's the good news. Developing a disruptive approach toward significantly improving the customer experience can be a lot of *fun*. It's actually easy to do. But it's different. Research and data absolutely validates the fact that this is the approach the best organizations on the planet are doing in reporting old-fashioned customer insights. They're completely disregarding the idea of the customer experience industrial monster, and the way they would like to sell you more data, more surveys, more tools, more mechanisms, more everything.

So let's get started with the process of building a holistic life support system for exceptional customer experience in your organization. I know that for many readers who are comfortable with the customer experience industrial monster, this may be a little hard to absorb because change is always hard.

THE SOS APPROACH

If you're starting from scratch, the best way to look at optimizing your organization for guaranteed success in customer experience is to use the SOS approach.

What is my Situation?

What are my Objectives?

What is my Strategy?

Ultimately, everything falls within the SOS approach.

Situation:
Customer Experience Innovation
Readiness Assessment

The best organizations today are starting with the real adult self-analysis, which we call a customer experience innovation readiness assessment.

Are we ready for this stuff? Do we have the culture? Do we have the budget? Do we have the vision? Do we have the tools? Do we have the _____ (fill in the blank)?

We really have to make sure that we've done the heavy lifting of looking at our situation. Do we have the right culture? Do we have the authority to make the changes?

One thing that's really surprising to me when it comes to what customers hate is just how institutionalized bad policies are. Wow! You look at hotels, you look at retailers, you look at just about everybody, and they have created these policies that can only be described as *punitive*. So one major requirement is this: Are you willing to walk away from the legacy of policies you've had for a long time that really punish your customer?

In order to get to the state of having happy customers, we must recognize that customers hate many of the things we do every single day, yet we ignore them. And that's why we've created the current state of hate. The current state of hate suggests that there are many things that your customers hate about you that you (1) either know and you're not willing to change, or (2) you haven't bothered to inquire about.

When you take a look at the architecture and structure of most surveys and promoter systems, they're designed to ask questions that, in legal terminology, are leading the witness. That's not going to get you anywhere. So the whole idea of taking your organization to another level is about making certain that you have a holistic approach to what is necessary in order to do this correctly.

Today we need to be agile, we need to be fast, and we need to be smart. But most importantly, we need to be *human*. We've done so much to try to institutionalize customer experience that we're at the fork in the road. We can choose the legacy road or the innovation road.

There is a philosophy that suggests there is no such thing as indecision. If you decide to do nothing, then what you've really decided to do is stick with your legacy approach. So the question is, are you willing to lean into the fun, excitement, and beauty that is customer experience innovation?

Objectives

Let's talk about the second phase of SOS. Once you've completed your readiness assessment, the next thing to do is ask yourself, "What are our objectives?"

It's okay to want to increase sales. It's okay to want to drive customer promotion. Of course, that's what we all want to do. None of that is bad at all. But if those are your *only* goals, you'll fail at this miserably. When you think about your objectives, remember that customer experience, and for that matter sales, are products of delivering exquisite value during the customer journey across a range of love/hate personas, in both digital and non-digital environments. That's the formula.

Be very careful as you put together your objectives to realize that your ability to do the things you want is a derivative of delivering value to the customer.

Strategy

Once you've completed the O of the SOS approach, it's time to build your strategy. We're going to talk about the framework of the strategy. But what I want to make certain I mention here is the fact that there is no one strategy that will work for every organization. It has to be specific to your culture, the size of your organization, the current state of happiness, and the training and expertise of your stakeholders. All of these many variables come into play.

You'll have to make certain you customize your strategy to make it real for your organization.

That's the starting point to get to customer experience innovation. What is our situation? Where are the gaps? What are our objectives? What do we really want to have happen? And what is our strategy?

A word of warning about strategy. We don't want to create "best practice" strategies. We want to create a strategy that is surgically connected to the enterprise goals and objectives. After all, the purpose of customer experience is to serve both the organization and the customer. You simply have to create surgical linkage between what the organization wants and what you're doing within your customer experience innovation. You also need to make sure you're open to the idea that the plan structure of customer experience innovation is very different than the way in which you've traditionally architected customer experience strategies.

One last note. I'm really surprised to see how many organizations have failed in the area of customer experience, and for that matter, have gone into bankruptcy, because they never bothered to create a customer experience strategy. Isn't that interesting? They plan everything: facilities, people, money, everything. But isn't it odd that one of the biggest causes of their failure is not delivering value to their customers? Yet these organizations literally never had anything that even resembled a customer experience point.

I hope this gives you a better sense of what customer experience innovation really is. Later, we'll get to the nuts and bolts of building out a plan that will allow you to deploy this in your organization in a very practical way.

TAKE ACTION!

Customers want value that is layered and dynamic. Layered value means you're going to give them more than they expected. Dynamic value means the value you deliver is constantly getting better.

The key to both is the constant innovation of new systems, products, and services that deliver value.

The best way to optimize your organization for guaranteed success in customer experience is to use the SOS approach, where you analyze your Situation, Objectives, and Strategy. This is how you build a holistic life support system for exceptional customer experience in your organization.

CHAPTER 12

HAPPINESS
AS A STRATEGY

Too many organizations assume that customer experience is something that is just simply robotically transacted by their organizational team, without regard to their culture. It turns out there's much more to the story. The best organizations have smartly institutionalized happiness in the form of Happiness as a Strategy (HaaS), and it actually works.

But it doesn't just work in terms of delivering incredible experiences to your customer. It also allows you to attract and keep the best talent, and significantly increase productivity, presenteeism, and employee yield. In short, the only way you can deliver exceptional customer experiences is to make *happiness an institutional priority.* When we love, respect, engage, and both collaborate with and support our teams, we create the life support system that makes customer experience real.

A culture of organizational happiness drives a culture of happy customers.

You've probably experienced a business where you can just feel the vibe of negativity. The culture is sick and the people are unhappy, and they can't wait to share the pain with their latest victim, also known as the customer. This is one of the big reasons why customer experience is failing within the majority of organizations in the world.

In a time of disruption and innovation, great organizations are reimagining the way they can use customer experience innovation to drive a happy organization that delivers exquisite customer experiences and quality of work life.

WHY ISN'T EVERYBODY TALKING ABOUT THIS?

After researching hundreds of books on customer experience, it's amazing to me that more experts aren't suggesting that the foundation of customer experience success is enterprise happiness. You don't need an advanced degree from an Ivy League college to know that unhappy people deliver unhappy experiences. Yet for some reason most organizations can't fathom the idea of using the word *happiness* as it relates to the organizational culture. In my consulting work, I've served organizations that have spent over $40 million on customer experience initiative while— astonishingly—investing *zero* dollars on quality of work life.

THE HIGH COST OF A TOXIC CULTURE

Let's cut to the bottom line: a healthy, positive company culture is a more profitable culture. This means that even if you're a miserly Scrooge who cares nothing about human feelings, you should at least *pretend* to care, because negativity sucks the profits from your balance sheet.

One cost is employee turnover. According to a 2019 report by SHRM on workplace culture, one in five Americans had left a job in the previous five years due to bad company culture. The cost of that turnover was an estimated $223 billion.

"Billions of wasted dollars," said SHRM president and CEO Johnny C. Taylor Jr., SHRM-SCP. "Millions of miserable people. It's not a warzone—it's the state of the American workplace. Toxicity itself isn't new. But now that we know the high costs and how managers can make workplaces better, there's no excuse for inaction."

The report, *The High Cost of a Toxic Workplace Culture*, found internal negativity created significant costs to companies in turnover and absenteeism; revealed indicators of toxic workplace cultures, such as harassment and discrimination; and highlighted the alarming impacts on employees. It found that 26 percent of employees surveyed say they *dreaded* going into work.[1]

Think about that. What if you had one hundred employees, and nearly one-third of them said they dreaded walking in the door every morning? How could those miserable people deliver amazing customer experiences? It can't happen. The only result will be what I call a "hatepoint farm," where the only crop is hatepoints sprouting like weeds everywhere you look.

You can look at company culture as a form of capital that can be either built up or squandered. In the *Harvard Business Review*, Kevin Stiroh, executive vice president and head of supervision at the Federal Reserve Bank of New York, wrote that insufficient "cultural capital" increases the possibility of employee misconduct, and must be seen as a form of risk just like liquidity risk or operational risk.

A company's cultural capital impacts what a firm produces, how it operates, and how it treats its customers. Cultural capital is just as important as physical capital (equipment, buildings, and property) and human capital (the accumulated knowledge and skills of workers), or reputational capital (like franchise value or brand recognition).

Investments in cultural capital are how you reduce that risk. Stiroh pointed out, "As with other forms of tangible and intangible capital, a firm must invest in cultural capital or it will deteriorate over time and adversely impact the firm's productive capacity."[2]

TOXICITY DESTROYS CUSTOMER EXPERIENCE

Customer experience requires that you eliminate what your *customers* hate so *you* can be the best option for attracting their purchasing dollars.

Likewise, the culture of happiness requires that you eliminate what *employees* hate so *you* are the best employment option for them. When you become their best option by respecting and honoring them, they will, in turn, serve your strategic initiatives and your customers.

Put more bluntly, there is no way you can deliver exquisite experiences to your customers until you're committed to doing the same for your employees. You need to create a positive company culture so that you'll (1) have employees who will happily deliver outstanding experiences to your customers, and (2) be able to attract and retain the very best employees—those who want to work only for an organization with a mission and culture they believe in.

UNHAPPY CULTURE = SICK EMPLOYEES

Unhappy cultures create stressful work environments, and stressful work environments result in an increase in healthcare costs by as much as 50 percent.

Research has shown a link between employee health and job performance, including workers in customer-facing roles. A growing body of evidence documents the relationship between a stressful work environment and a range of chronic conditions, including depression, hypertension, and sleeping problems.

A 2019 study by Colonial Life found that more than 20 percent of workers spend more than five hours on the clock each week thinking about their stressors and worries. An additional 50 percent of workers reported losing between one and five hours of work to stress each week.

Citing statistics from the US Bureau of Labor Statistics, Colonial Life concluded that with 128.5 million full-time employees earning on average $21 per hour, workers who are disengaged or unproductive because of stress are costing employers billions of dollars.[3]

NEED MORE EVIDENCE OF HOW A BAD CULTURE BREEDS HATEPOINTS? OK . . .

In case you're not yet convinced, here are some other nasty ways a toxic culture can drag down your organization:

- **Kills your brand reputation as an employer.** Unhappy cultures repel great talent. Glassdoor ratings and employee word-of-mouth are central to acquiring exceptional talent. Exceptional talent is required for exceptional customer experience.

Organizations with a negative culture can enter into a vicious downward spiral. Bad cultures of unhappiness *attract more bad people*. Bad people deliver bad experiences, both internally and externally. Customers respond poorly to the experience, which helps feed the negativity that is the culture that attracts more bad people, and so it goes.

- **Kills innovation.** Unhappy cultures stifle innovation due to the simple fact that stakeholders refuse to collaborate with both customers and leadership. Without this collaboration, your innovation pipeline will dry up.

- **Makes inclusion and diversity impossible.** The entire premise of inclusion and diversity is the ability for an organization to treat all of their employees equitably and with respect. I've never seen an example of an unhappy culture that has truly put diversity and inclusion first.

HOW TO GET HAPPY

HaaS requires a thoughtful and measured approach. The following is a framework for building a strong and effective happiness strategy within your organization.

- **Happiness mission statement.** While your "normal" mission statement is aimed outward, at your market, your happiness mission statement needs to be aimed inward, toward your organization and its stakeholders. Taking good care of your employees is just as important as taking care of your customers. After all, your employees are the ones who create the value that attracts, delights, and keeps your customers. You need a mission statement describing the culture you want to create.

- **Specific happiness goals.** Yes, happiness can be measured. Perhaps not directly, but in its effects on employee behavior. Some key employee happiness metrics include the employee turnover rate, absenteeism, productivity, mistakes made, and customer complaints. Find out what they are today, and set goals to improve them by set points in the future. Remember, you cannot "buy" employee happiness with cheap gimmicks such as handing out gift cards to Starbucks. Your company culture must be genuine and deeply rooted in your everyday interactions.

- **Measurements beyond surveys.** Employee surveys are just about as useful as most customer surveys: that is, they are useless. According to a study by Officevibe, 70 percent of employees don't respond to annual engagement surveys, and nearly 30 percent think the surveys are a waste of time. To make it worse, 80 percent of employees don't believe managers will act on survey data.[4]

    Companies should look at using "micropulses" (a few questions focused on a particular topic) and key touchpoints to sense how employees are feeling. In this way, companies can maximize insights while simultaneously minimizing the use of employee time.

Continuous feedback means continuous *listening*, and should translate to continuous action. Employee happiness levels can be gauged by listening to employees' signals, using the subsequent insights to take action, and then communicating back to employees that action has been taken. For employees, a particular source of unhappiness is their belief that management will take a new idea submitted by an employee, and then appropriate it as their own. That's a sure way to generate a truckload of hatepoints!

- **Find out what your employees hate.** Yes, this can be painful, especially if you—the leader—are identified as being a source of hatepoints. It takes a thick skin to log onto Glassdoor and read what some of your employees have to say. But it's always better to bring issues out into the open.

  You need to consider that your employees may be reluctant to disagree with you out of fear of retribution. Many companies have a forced "happy" culture that boasts of "open communication" as a corporate value while managers discourage dissenting opinions. Open communication is built on a foundation of *trust*. First comes trust, then comes truth.

- **Eliminate what your employees hate.** This is the moment of truth when your employees will say, "Just as we thought! We make suggestions, and the boss ignores them." Or they will say, "Wow! We made a suggestion, and the boss listened!" Ideas are useless unless followed by action. If you're not going to respond to your employees, then don't even ask them. But you should ask them, and you should respond, even if only to say, "Thank you, but we can't do what you ask. But we appreciate the suggestion."

- **Find out what your employees love.** This is the flip side to finding out what they hate. But it's important that you don't waste your time and money on initiatives that your employees may not care about.

  For example, as Nishal Mistri from Curious Thing noted, an increasing number of employers are turning to cheap perks like free food, beer fridges, Ping-Pong tables, and bean bag chairs in offices, with the idea that these things will deliver a positive workplace experience, particularly for younger employees.

  Fully 40 percent of business owners believe employees value these office perks. But research revealed that very few employees, in *any* demographic, view benefits such as Ping-Pong tables (5 percent) or company outings (9 percent) as valuable to their workforce experience. More than half of respondents (53 percent) reported that having games in the office is a distraction, and actually decreases productivity.[5]

- **Implement new innovations that your employees will love.** Your employees are no different from your customers: They want to see and experience new things that will help them do their jobs better. New tools, new strategies, new ways of solving problems—they want them! What they do *not* want is change that makes *your* job easier while making *their* job more difficult. Don't get the bright idea that asking your employees to fill out a new report or questionnaire is going to make them happy. It isn't.

- **Develop a center for employee happiness (CEH).** No, I'm not talking about a refurbished break room with a Ping-Pong table and free bagels every Friday. Obviously, if you're a small business, the CEH is going to be located in your office. You will be the chief happiness officer (CHO) as you "manage by walking around." But in a big company, the salary you pay your designated full-time CHO will more than pay for itself in increased productivity and lower employee turnover and absenteeism. The secondary effect will be to produce fewer hatepoints and more lovepoints from your customers, who will respond to interacting with a happier, more engaged group of frontline employees.

- **Host employee listening sessions.** These should be very casual, with small groups. Frankly, you should be listening *every day*, but on a regular basis you need to gather people together for an open discussion. What are we doing right? What are we doing not so well? Where are we behind schedule, and how can we fix that? The atmosphere must be nonjudgmental and honest, with low expectations—in other words, it's just as bad to over-promise as it is to be aloof and detached.

- **Create an enterprise social channel to collaborate around happiness.** Digital platforms for meetings have come a long way in a short period of time. Enterprise social software is used by large organizations to improve their collaboration and social networking. Comprising corporate social networks (intranet) as well as other social networking software, the person-to-person connections it creates can boost the communication, productivity, and time management of a company. But while collaboration can often lead to fresh ideas and greater return on investment, it can also be tricky to pull off. You need to spell out who is in charge of what, and the tools you should be using to share the load.

- **Create and launch a happiness innovation challenge.** An innovation challenge or hackathon is a way to involve the entire company or a group in generating innovative ideas or challenges that could positively impact customers or employees. Often the best innovations emerge through teams addressing unsolved problems. Creating a culture of happiness is no different. The structure of a happiness culture can often emerge from a "brainstorming" session, in which participants are encouraged to express what would make them happy at work, regardless of how crazy the idea might sound.

- **Develop and deploy a formal Happiness as a Strategy plan.** I put this at the end of the list because it should be the culmination of everything that has gone before. It must include time-tested strategies as well as new innovations. It must include as many ideas as possible offered by the employees that will help them be happy and productive, and create memorable touchpoints for their customers. It must be sustainable and supported by adequate investment

    The plan should be deployed with measurements and be designed for continuous improvement.

• • •

ZOOM:
THE HAPPY (AND PROFITABLE) COMPANY

There's a list for everything—including the companies where the employees are the happiest.

Comparably.com is a company dedicated to making workplaces transparent and rewarding for both employees and employers. It seeks to reveal company cultures and market compensation (as contributed by real employees), and showcases the most fair and accurate display of employer brands. In its 2020 list of the Top 100 Highest-Rated Companies with the Happiest Employees, these were the top five large companies:

1. Zoom Video Communications (San Jose, California)

2. HubSpot (Cambridge, Massachusetts)

3. Microsoft (Redmond, Washington)

4. RingCentral (Belmont, California)

5. Apple (Cupertino, California)[6]

We've all heard of Microsoft and Apple. But Zoom Video Communications? It's the company that offers the videoconferencing services that have become ubiquitous. The name has become a verb, as in, "Let's Zoom at one o'clock with the team." It's only fitting that Zoom should be number one in employee happiness, because when you go to their website, the "About" page says, "We deliver happiness. The greatest, most sustainable happiness comes from making others happy. It is our privilege to deliver you happiness every single day."

The mission of Zoom is: "Make video communications frictionless and secure."

Their vision: "Video communications empowering people to accomplish more."

Their value: "Care—Community, Customers, Company, Teammates, Selves."

Their culture: "Delivering happiness."

With those kinds of proclamations, the company had better be a super-happy place to work. The employees are called "Zoomies," and their website has a series of employee testimonials. For example, Jeff Koll, who is the head of the European Center of Excellence, says, "You know what I love about Zoom? It's constant growth, constant fun, and constant change. I work with the smartest and best people that I could ever be surrounded with!"

This culture of love transfers to their customers and industry analysts:

- *Inc.* magazine named Zoom one of its Best Workplaces for 2020.

- Let's Do Video voted Zoom a 2019 LDV Readers' Choice Awards Winner.

- Glassdoor rated Zoom the #2 Best Place to Work in 2019.

- Frost & Sullivan named Zoom their 2019 Company of the Year for the Global Video Conferencing Industry.[7]

There are many more.

This relentless embrace of happiness has led to robust growth and impressive profits. Eric Yuan, a former Cisco engineer and executive, founded Zoom in 2011, and launched its software in

2013. Zoom's rapid revenue growth and perceived ease-of-use and reliability of its software resulted in a $1 billion valuation in 2017, making it a "unicorn" company. The company first became profitable in 2019, and completed an initial public offering that year. Zoom joined the NASDAQ-100 stock index on April 30, 2020. In that same year, the nine-year-old company posted revenues of $2.65 billion with $660 million in operating income.

Happiness can be very profitable!

TAKE ACTION!

If you embrace the idea that if you reduce the hatepoints felt by your *customers*, they will reward you with their credit cards, then you should also embrace the idea that if you reduce the hatepoints felt by your *employees*, they will reward you with greater productivity, lower attrition, higher engagement, and better customer relations. Statistics show that unhappy employees are more expensive to a company than are happy employees, even after figuring the investment cost of Happiness as a Strategy (HaaS).

Analyze all of your employee engagement data, and then make a plan to improve each data point by 10 percent every year. For example, if the average customer-facing employee works in their position for two years and six months before leaving the company, then set a new goal of two years and nine months, then three years. What do you need to do to keep them happier longer?

CHAPTER 13

THE CUSTOMER SURVEY
IS YOUR ENEMY

For the past fifty years, companies have been trained to believe they need customer surveys that purportedly provide accurate, actionable information on how customers feel. The rationale is that in order to find out what customers think, you only need to ask them, and they will honestly tell you.

To some extent this is true, but the assumption is sufficiently flawed to call into question the entire concept. Unless crafted and presented carefully, a customer survey will not be your friend but your enemy.

Before we dive into the pros and cons of customer surveys— and how they can be made better—let's take a look at how they're often constructed.

While surveys come in many forms, the most common is the one devised in 1932 by an American social psychologist named Rensis Likert. In his survey format, the respondent is presented not with a question but with a statement, to which he or she responds by choosing one of five answers on a scale. For scoring purposes, the answers may be given a numerical value:

1	2	3	4	5
Disagree strongly	Disagree	Undecided	Agree	Agree strongly

For statements that have a common theme—for example, customer service—if you ask the customer for a series of responses, then you can add up the scores and arrive at an overall score.

You can also take the survey results from many customers and add up their responses to each individual question. Let's say, for example, you present the statement "The website was easy to navigate" to 100 customers, and the average response is "disagree" (or a score of 2). In this case, you're supposed to learn that your website navigation needs to be improved.

Surveys can also take the form of a series of questions. Survey questions can use either a closed-ended or open-ended format to collect answers from individuals. A closed-ended question includes a predefined list of answer options, while an open-ended question asks the respondent to provide an answer in their own words. For large-scale surveys, closed-ended questions are used. Only for small groups where you want to dig deeply would you attempt to use open-ended questions.

The use of these surveys seems scientific, and it's very easy for managers to conduct such surveys, look at the results, and then write a memo to the relevant department asking them to fix the problem. The challenge is that the results are fragmentary and highly subjective, and are a poor indicator of whether the customer will choose your company again from the available options. As this book has revealed, customers can hate you or some aspect of your service, and still choose you over your competitor.

But that's a fool's paradise because the minute a savvy newcomer enters the market, your customers will drop you like a rock.

For many reasons, customer surveys can provide data that either isn't useful or is even misleading. Let's look at the most common problems.

SURVEYS ARE TOO LONG

Recently I was on my mobile phone company's website to make a change in my plan. The procedure itself was relatively painless, and took just a few minutes. So far, so good! As I was leaving, a pop-up appeared and asked if I wanted to take a customer satisfaction survey. Okay, I thought, why not? So I clicked "yes."

The first question appeared. Am I male, female, or other? Ah— they wanted to begin with demographic data. With a sigh and a glance at the clock—I had a conference call in ten minutes—I clicked "male." Then it asked me which age group I was in. This is irrelevant nonsense, I thought as I skipped the question. Then it asked for my income range. No way! I skipped that one, too. It asked how often I used my phone, and if it was more for business or pleasure. Those questions required too much thinking. I was in a hurry, and I skipped them, too.

Then the questions began about my customer experience. These were multiple choice, with responses ranked on a Likert scale from 1 (disagree strongly) to 5 (agree strongly). The first question was, "The website is easy to navigate." I don't know! Compared to what? I clicked 4, "agree."

The next question was, "I was able to find what I needed." Yes, I was able to get my business done . . . so again I clicked 4, "agree." Why? Because clicking 5, "strongly agree," seemed too enthusiastic. I didn't want them to think everything was perfect. I wanted to keep a little in reserve.

This went on for a few more questions until, with my eye on the relentless tick-tock of the clock, I bailed out. I didn't finish the survey. I had neither the time nor the patience.

A study by Interaction Metrics discovered that, despite good intentions of improving customer happiness and overall experience, retailers are largely wasting customers' time—and their own—by conducting customer satisfaction surveys that are too long. Of the several dozen retailer surveys they studied, they found the average consisted of twenty-three questions—far too many!

It's one reason why, despite retailers' desperation to "engage" with their customers, the response rates are low and continue to drop. Customers are simply worn out by so much interaction! Many brands today see a response rate of just 2 percent, producing data that is fragmentary and marginally accurate.[1]

This is a symptom of two growing problems. One is "survey request fatigue," when people have been asked for their feedback so often they refuse to respond. Survey request fatigue causes people to ignore the request for feedback and reduces survey return rates.

The other is "survey taking fatigue," when the subject is in the middle of a survey and gets tired of the questions. This can diminish the quality of their responses because they'll skip questions, quickly check boxes just to get it done, or to abandon the survey completely.

SURVEYS ARE INTRUSIVE

Not long after my friend Jane had bought her new luxury car, the phone call came. Looking at the caller ID, she saw it was from the dealership. She assumed it was something important—some detail about the car or the sale that she needed to know—so she picked it up. A cheerful person named Tom was on the line. He asked if she had a few minutes. Sure, she replied. The questions began. Was she satisfied with her new car? Was she given a tour of the service department? Did she feel as though she fully understood the contract? Was the waiting room satisfactory, and did she notice the free coffee and doughnuts? Tom asked her to rank each question from 1 (very poor) to 5 (excellent). After a few minutes of this, Jane became impatient. "Look," she said, "everything was great. Just perfect. If I have any issues, trust me, I'll call you. I have to go to a meeting. Thanks."

"We're almost done—just a few more questions," replied Tom. "I know you're busy. How likely are you to recommend our dealership to a friend or family member?"

"Three!" Jane spat into the phone. An answer of "three" meant "fair."

"Oh?" replied Tom. "A three. All right. Can you tell me why you said 'three'?"

"What?" said Jane. "No—no—sorry, I meant five. It was a *five*. Everything was *perfect*! Listen, Tom, I've really got to go. Have a great day."

Exasperated, she hung up. In reality, Jane felt that at the closing the manager had tried too hard to upsell her on an extended warranty, various options, and other items that Jane knew were nothing more than strategies to get more money out of her. She had agreed to buy the car, but before the sale was final the dealer tried to jack up the price. Jane had stood firm and the sale was made, but the arm-twisting had left her irritated.

The net result? The survey call had been annoying and lowered her perception of the dealership. And throughout the customer journey and all the touchpoints, the *one thing* Jane hated was her encounter with the manager who had put the hard sell on her. That hatepoint was never expressed in the telephone survey. The company would never know about it. Instead, all the company saw was Tom's tabulations and his report that the customer had given Northside Luxury Autos five stars.

(By the way, new-car dealerships are granted local monopolies by the automakers. Jane's car dealer was located twenty minutes from her home. If she decided she hated them, the next closest showroom was in the next town, over an hour away. No matter how much Jane hated Northside Luxury Autos, there was little chance she would abandon them and drive over an hour to another one.)

This type of insistent outreach to customers is one example of the increasingly widespread corporate practice of digging for customer opinions and dumping them into a quantitative data set. Although many marketing managers see it as harvesting the thoughts of customers, others see customer service surveys as a source of awkward interactions with irritated customers who provide bad data.

SURVEYS DON'T REACH THE PEOPLE YOU WANT

My friend Jane is a busy person. She runs a business and has a family, and her schedule is tight. She hasn't got a lot of free time. When Tom called, she was willing to give him a few minutes. After all, she's in business, and she likes getting customer feedback. She knows how valuable it can be, if used properly. But when the survey dragged on and started eating into her time, she cut it short.

Northside Luxury Autos was left with a survey that was worse than useless. It gave the managers an inaccurate picture of Jane's experience.

The sad fact is that Jane is *precisely* the type of customer whom the company should want to hear from. She's relatively young, affluent, and knowledgeable about cars. She chose her new car because she believed in the brand, and would probably do so again in a few years. She's not a "brand-jumper." Once she likes a brand, she sticks with it. But she doesn't have time to submit to lengthy surveys. She's just too busy. As a result, her opinion will not be heard.

Who, then, has time to respond to surveys? The answer is people who have time on their hands. People who are unemployed or minimally employed, don't have a busy family schedule, or are retired. There's nothing wrong with such people, but they aren't the ideal target customer for a premium auto brand whose cars sell for $50,000 and up.

If a business calls a landline number and gets an answer, and the respondent has ten minutes to spare right at that moment, what does that tell you about them? They might be a nice person, but unless you're selling supplemental Medicare plans, they may not be the ideal survey subject.

As far as telephone surveys are concerned, in the past few decades their contact rate, effectiveness, and reliability have been dropping. Pew Research is in the business of conducting telephone surveys, and the nonprofit reports that in 1997, the typical telephone survey response rate was 36 percent. By 2018, it had plummeted to just 6 percent. Their research showed that the same pattern was being experienced across the industry.

The nonprofit pinpointed a number of reasons why response rates are declining.

- **Robocalls.** The volume of robocalls has skyrocketed, reaching an estimated 3.4 billion per month in 2019. For many years, cell phones were immune to robocalls, but that's changing. Since public opinion polls typically appear as an unknown or unfamiliar number, they are easily mistaken for telemarketing appeals. And the use of phony caller IDs, in which robocalls appear to come from a familiar local number, have further conditioned recipients to ignore calls unless they are certain of their origin.

- **Spam technologies.** Survey calls from legitimate sources can be erroneously tagged as "spam." Numerous cellular carriers, third-party apps, and cell phone operating systems block incoming phone numbers or warn users that incoming numbers are from potential fraudsters.

For companies conducting surveys, these new challenges add to a long-standing set of reasons why many people won't respond, including concerns over intrusions on their time and privacy, people feeling too busy to participate, and a general lack of interest in taking surveys.[2]

SURVEYS ARE TOO SIMPLISTIC

Some surveys are extremely simplistic.

The Net Promoter Score (NPS) is a proprietary instrument developed by Fred Reichheld, who owns the registered NPS trademark in conjunction with Bain & Company and Satmetrix.

As an answer to the complexity and intrusiveness of the traditional questionnaire, the NPS asks one simple question: "How likely is it that you will recommend the company to a friend or colleague?"

There are three possible answers to that question: "Yes," "No," "Not quite sure." It's one question with one of three answer choices. The question is obvious and the answers are clear. This is the type of question you can literally ask a customer as they are walking out the door or leaving your website. The idea is that your customer will have given his or her feedback spontaneously, without thinking, rather than sift their way through a long set of ready-made questions.

The answer puts a company's customer into one of three categories: Promoters, Detractors, and Passives. If you want to survey vast numbers of customers in a short amount of time, I suppose this is a good way to do it. While's its simplicity is admirable, the NPS does not tell management teams anything about *what's working* and *what must improve*. It does not provide any actionable information.

In addition, with this metric, timing is important. At what point in the customer journey is the question asked? Is the business surveying the customer after an extremely unfortunate mishap, or after he or she takes advantage of a generous company policy?

Let's say you own a big office supply store. You survey 200 customers per day who come in and out of your store. At the end of a six-day week, after 1,200 customers, your NPS is this: Yes = 579, No = 368, Not quite sure = 253.

What does that tell you? It tells you that roughly 48 percent of the respondents would recommend your store to a friend. The other 52 percent would not, or aren't sure.

But what does that *mean*?

To be honest, it means *nothing*. It does not provide any actionable information. Of those 52 percent who would not recommend your store to a friend, or aren't sure, do you know *why* they feel that way? Is it your products? Your sales staff? Your store layout? The music you play in your store? A long line at the checkout counter? The fact is, having been informed that there's some level of hate for your store, even if you wanted to take corrective action, you would have no idea where to begin.

According to D. Randall Brandt, vice president at Maritz Research, while NPS may have some predictive capacity for broad customer populations, it says little about what motivates individual purchasing choices. Additionally, knowing the overall NPS doesn't give any information about the makeup of the promoter and detractor populations. Because of this, the NPS has little to offer management teams in the way of actionable next steps.[3]

Imagine, if you will, if Comcast, which I profiled earlier in the book, had relied exclusively on the NPS system when tackling its customer experience problem. From NPS, it would have learned this from its customers: "I think your company sucks." That would be all. Nothing more. Having heard this sentiment from millions of customers, it would have been up to the company to figure out *why* their customers hated them. Was it the customer service? The fees? The quality of the programming? The features available on the remote control? No one in the company would know because the customers had never been asked.

The moral of the story is that there are *no shortcuts* to creating exceptional customer experiences. There are no one-size-fits-all solutions. There is no easy "fix it" button. It's an ongoing, never-ending process that requires the participation of everyone who takes a paycheck from your company.

RELIABILITY AND VALIDITY
ARE TWO DIFFERENT THINGS

A survey can have a high level of reliability and generate consistent responses year after year. This can lead managers to believe that since the survey produces a *reliable* set of data, then it must be *valid*.

They are two different things.

Validity relates to whether the survey questions truly measure issues of importance to the company, and the degree to which the survey measures what it claims to measure.

There are many types of validity. One of the most important is *construct validity*, which refers to the extent to which a survey actually measures what it's supposed to. In the world of commerce, for example, a customer survey must produce information pertaining to two key questions: "How likely are you to purchase from us again? How likely are you to recommend us to a friend?" Any questions that don't support those outcomes are likely to be wasted and serve only to annoy the customer. For example, the car dealership asked Jane if the dealership was conveniently located. This was an irrelevant and silly question because the next nearest dealer was located over an hour away.

When response data from a survey with low validity is plotted on a graph, it doesn't form the normal distribution shape of a bell curve where most data is near the middle. Instead, it will show scattered responses with large numbers at extreme ends of the scale. Such widely dispersed responses suggest the questions may not be properly structured.

The goal of the organization using the questionnaire or survey is to get a clear picture of how the customer *feels* about their experience. Such surveys measure the self-reported attitudes, opinions, or behaviors of the respondents. These are what psychologists call *constructs*. Because constructs are complex and intangible human characteristics or behaviors, they are difficult to assess by any single question. They are more effectively measured by asking a series of related questions relevant to a variety of aspects of the topic, such as customer satisfaction. The responses to these individual but related questions can then be combined to form a score or scale measure along a continuum.

This scientific approach works well with subjects who have been enlisted into a research study and accept the time commitment required. They may be willing to answer dozens of questions that, to the test-taker, may seem redundant. But customer surveys are very different. Your customer has just paid his or her money for your product or service, and now you ask that same customer to give you a "freebie" by spending ten or fifteen minutes completing a detailed customer satisfaction survey. Sorry, but most customers will say, "You've got my money—that's not enough? Now you want me to give you free advice on how to run your business? No thank you."

Sometimes it may seem as though getting actionable information from your customers is like gazing into a crystal ball on a foggy day. The information may be in there somewhere, but you're not going to see it. The answer? Throw away the crystal ball. It's not the tool you need. It's too easy. There is no facile, low-investment method to learn what's in the hearts of your customers. To get on the right track, you need to do two things: make customer intelligence a business priority, and use the right tools for collecting it.

TAKE ACTION!

Collect all of your current methods of taking surveys and throw them in the trash can. Then read the next chapter.

CHAPTER 14

REALRATINGS:
THE CUSTOMER SURVEY OF TOMORROW

Having pointed out the significant flaws in many customer surveys, we need to return to the central question: How do you learn what your customers think about your brand, product, or experience? What do they love about it or hate about it? And given how they feel about your brand—both love and hate—what might they do about that? And what should *you* do about it?

There must be a way to get honest, spontaneous, actionable information from your customers. The more you think about it, the more it seems that all roads lead to customer surveys. Okay, let's face it: Customer surveys are here to stay. There is simply no other way to ask the customer for their opinion than to . . . well . . . *ask* them.

* * *

HOW TO USE SURVEYS EFFECTIVELY

Despite the challenges of surveys, you can use them—whether online or by phone—to get good, actionable opinions from your customers. Here's what you need to do.

Keep It Simple, Stupid! (KISS)

You've seen the somewhat overused KISS acronym before. I'm using it now because it especially applies to customer surveys.

The #1 rule of voluntary customer surveys, where you ask the customer without any forewarning, "Hey, please take our survey," is that *it must be brief*. It must include no more than a handful of questions. It must take the customer no longer than two minutes to complete. The questions must be closed-ended and multiple choice.

Remember, your customer is giving you their time. Let's say your customer is a lawyer who charges $240 an hour. If you ask her to take a survey of five minutes in duration, you're asking her to give you twenty dollars. Cut that down to two minutes, and you're asking her to give you eight dollars. Be respectful of her valuable time!

You have a brief window of opportunity to keep your customer focused on your survey. In an OpinionLab study, 52 percent of respondents indicated they would likely abandon a survey after just three minutes. Even if people make it past three minutes, the quality of survey responses tends to rapidly diminish as the respondents hurry through to the end. Keeping your questions brief and simple to understand is the best way to combat this kind of response fatigue.[1]

Always let people know how many questions there are up front. Write your questions so that the respondent can quickly answer them spontaneously, without thinking. For example, the question "Do you always buy organic food?" creates a barrier because it contains an absolute ("always"). This forces the respondent to think: "Have I *ever* bought non-organic food? Are canned tomatoes organic? How about bananas?" This question is certain to elicit a meaningless answer. But if you ask, "Do you *prefer* to buy organic food?" the answer will be immediate—"yes" or "no."

Ensure the Questions Are Important and Valid

Because you are asking just a few questions, you need to ensure they are both important to your mission and valid. You cannot ask every question you'd like to! Surveys are often created by committees representing various departments within a company. Sales wants to know if the customer was pleased by the sales process. Fulfillment wants to know if the product was delivered on time. The brand manager wants to know if the product met the customer's expectations. Everyone has their pet concern. You need to remember that *the customer does not care about your problems.* Most customers are happy to be asked their opinion, but they don't want to be unpaid management consultants.

Questions that are too broad provide a vague impression of customer displeasure or satisfaction, but don't give you actionable information. Asking a customer to rate their experience from 1 to 5 does not tell you the exact problem.

Give Your Customer a Reward

When you ask a customer to participate in a survey, you're asking them to provide two things of value—their time and their opinion. You don't give away products for free, so why should your customers give you free stuff? Reward them with a gift card, a discount, entry into a sweepstake, or something else that's easy and fun. Offering an appealing incentive has been shown to boost response rates and completion rates. It can also strengthen relationships with customers and encourage them to remain involved, as it shows your appreciation for their time and effort.

I'm Afraid to Ask You This . . .

I'm sure you've heard the phrase. "I'm afraid to ask you this . . ." It's a real phenomenon that individuals don't want to ask certain questions because they're afraid of a stark and accurate answer.

When your doctor walks into the exam room with your blood panel and a somber look on his face, you may pause for a moment and say, "I'm afraid to ask . . ."

When your romantic interest says, "We need to talk," you're afraid to ask what it's about, knowing that the breakup is impending. Unfortunately, we've baked this fear of hearing unpleasant truths into the way in which we manage consumer insights, and for too many organizations it can lead to disaster.

Many traditional surveys are designed to elicit positive responses. People often try to be polite, and tell the survey sponsors what they think the sponsors want to hear. For example, let's say you launch a new software product. Users who can't get it to work properly may be unwilling to admit it, even if the software instructions or design are flawed. They may be willing to blame themselves for not being smart enough to catch on, and tell you it works just fine so they don't feel stupid.

Some people don't want to appear out of step with their peers. There was a case involving unisex bathrooms at Williams College, which went co-ed in 1970. As mTab.com reported, a survey taken among the students showed support for the idea of unisex bathrooms in a freshman dorm. But once the unisex bathroom was established, students quickly found it awkward and uncomfortable. Students voted to return to the previous separate bathroom arrangement, with most of them claiming they had been against the idea from the beginning. They had only agreed so they wouldn't appear old-fashioned or uncool.[2]

Debbie Downer Strikes Again

Customers can be weird about how they reply to surveys. Some people are eager to trash your company and your effort just because that's the way they are. They have a negative worldview, and nothing pleases them. They enjoy putting you down because it makes them feel important. This is why no matter what you do, you'll get a certain percentage of people who say you suck.

Some survey respondents want to make themselves out better than, more than, or somehow superior to others. Others may be unwilling to disclose something about their beliefs or nature they don't want others to know. Some may be embarrassed by a question, finding it easier to lie than admit a truth they may find shameful. Similar to becoming defensive, people may lie on surveys when they're afraid their honest opinion is not necessarily mainstream or politically correct, a concept known as social desirability bias.

You cannot allow such people to discourage you from seeking opinions from your customers.

To Get Accurate Answers, You Need to Ask the Right Questions

The survey and questionnaire industry has run amok. It has developed a symbiotic relationship between organizations seeking positive feedback and a survey industry that is glad to provide skewed positive data. I'm sure this co-creation will continue with many organizations until they finally become desperate enough to ask the tough questions.

Over the last few decades, I have developed a system that is designed to get to a net rating that uses linguistics that increase the likelihood for accurate customer feedback. This survey approach provides far better insights about the way in which a customer feels about their experience and ultimately your brand.

This is why—as I'll reveal in the pages ahead—I advocate that you use the RealRatings system to mine accurate, actionable information.

THE THREE DIMENSIONS OF CUSTOMER SATISFACTION

Businesses do surveys for the purpose of gaining insights, but few use them to invent better experiences. I have audited surveys of clients to find that there were hundreds of surveys in their survey pile where the customer absolutely hated them for good reasons and there was no system in place to take those insights and to (1) make the customer happy and (2) use what they learned to invent better experiences. The problem of not using customer insights is epidemic. There is a general assumption that we're doing good customer experience work by simply pushing out surveys. Most of them are really structured to make the organization feel that their customers like them more than they do.

In my experience, many organizations actually know how bad they are at various touchpoints, but they don't want to memorialize the problem through a properly structured satisfaction rating program. If you really want to eliminate the hatepoints and install the lovepoints, you simply need to look at the three dimensions of customer happiness.

Dimension 1:
The Four Customer Personas

You do not serve a singular customer. You serve a range of customer personas that can be distinguished not by age or race or how they dress, but by their individual loves and hates. In this book, I've presented the four basic types. Across the range of customer personas there's a well-established set of hatepoints and lovepoints. In order to understand how to serve *all* of your customers, you need to know what customers hate and love across your four customer personas. I'll discuss this important point in much greater detail in the pages ahead.

Dimension 2:
The Customer Touchpoint Journey

You serve each customer across five well-defined touchpoints, and you must glean insights about their complete journey in order to determine where there are hatepoints and lovepoints. Most organizations survey the customer specific to just a few touchpoints.

Dimension 3:
The Net Customer Experience

Most customer rating systems are afraid to ask the hate questions, or they structure questions that have a neutral response. In order to get to an actionable customer experience rating—the RealRatings system—you have to find out what the customer hated and subtract that from what the customer loved.

RealRatings surveys are custom architected to address the uniqueness of the experience and to select the proper linguistics in order to glean accurate responses. This provides you with two very significant improvements in terms of customer experience insights. First, it provides far better insights as to what the customer did *not* like, so as to provide a net experience that is far more accurate, although perhaps less flattering. The second benefit is that these insights will allow you to extinguish hatepoints through new innovations while optimizing the lovepoints.

The sum total of the customer personas' experience over the five touchpoints—which may extend in time to cover many years—is the Net Customer Experience (NCX), or RealRating.

This is the measurement of what the customer hated and loved across the five touchpoints and a range of hate/love personas.

Hatepoints are measured across four negative experiences, from 1 (not good) to 4 (really hated).

Lovepoints are measured across four positive experiences, from 1 (unliked) to 4 (really loved).

Note that in both cases there is no middle fifth choice of "undecided" or "not sure."

The RealRating is the total of hatepoints subtracted from the lovepoints. I purposely designed this patent pending program to not be a five-point survey, as neutrality—in other words, having a point in the middle that is neutral—makes it easy for the customer to avoid answering the question by choosing the bland middle ground.

The RealRating represents the net total of what the experience was like for customers by subtracting the hatepoints from the lovepoints to produce a score. This score is very useful because it's expressly asking what a customer didn't like and what a customer did like at a specific touchpoint. This provides actionable insights that an organization can use to rapidly fix the dislikes to significantly improve their RealRatings NCX score.

THE FOUR CUSTOMER PERSONAS

Earlier in the book, I revealed the four customer personas. They are the Driver, the Analytical, the Amiable, and the Collaborator. Each persona brings their own set of expectations to the interactions or touchpoints with your brand.

For example, the Driver knows what she wants and expects prompt, efficient, no-nonsense service. She isn't looking for validation or friendship, and will quickly pile on the hate if her expectations are not met.

In contrast, the Amiable is the polar opposite of the Driver. This customer wants you to be their friend. They want you to understand them and why they want the product or service. They want a high level of personal service. These are the people who will famously spend half an hour chatting on the phone with the Zappos customer service rep before ordering one pair of shoes.

The Collaborator needs the consensus of a group or partner in order to proceed. The collaborator is the man who will say, "I like it, but I need to talk to my partner before we buy."

The Analytical needs to know every detail of the product or service. Remember the old joke about the person who goes to a restaurant and, before ordering the chicken, interrogates the server about the type of chicken, the farm it came from, how it was raised, and if it were slaughtered humanely? That's the Analytical.

Of course, there are shades of each—for example, a Driver may show some characteristics of the Collaborator—but as a foundation, the system works very well.

These personas each view your company through a different lens. They literally see your salespeople differently from the others. If asked to describe your company, the Driver might say, "Oh, that's the place with the super-efficient sales team." The Analytical might say, "That's the company with the super-informative sales team. They really know their products." The Amiable might say your staff is exceptionally friendly and welcoming ("They serve you free coffee!"), while the Collaborator appreciates your patience and lack of pressure.

And guess what? They're all talking about the same sales staff! This is possible because the customer-facing employees have been carefully trained to adapt their behavior to match or mirror that of the customer. They know how to pivot to meet the expectation of each customer persona.

The critically important fact that most customer service surveys ignore, and cannot measure, is that *each persona has a different set of loves and hates.* The chatty salesperson will be hated by the Driver and loved by the Amiable. The fast and efficient salesperson will be hated by the Analytical, who wants to spend time gathering information, but loved by the Driver, who wants to waste no time. The website that's full of customer testimonials will be loved by the Collaborator, who wants to show them to his partner, but may be off-putting to the Analytical, who's looking for facts, not a sales pitch.

There will always be some common ground among the four personas. For example, if you sell a defective product, they will all hate it, and rightfully so. If you promise two-day delivery and the item arrives five days later, they'll all hate it. But across the entire duration of the customer journey from touchpoint to touchpoint, you're competing on the basis of customer service, and it's your service that will make your customer either love you or hate you.

The problem is that different people have different ideas about what constitutes customer service they love. It's all about the fulfillment of customer expectations. Look at it in its simplest terms. Let's say you go to a five-star restaurant and order filet mignon, and your waiter instead brings you lobster thermidor. You're going to be angry! It doesn't matter how delicious the lobster thermidor might be, it's not what you expected. The same thing applies to the customer experience across every touchpoint. The Driver will expect a seamless, no-nonsense set of interactions, and if she doesn't get it, then she'll be upset. The Amiable will expect a leisurely, chatty interaction, and if he doesn't get it, he'll be disappointed.

YOU NEED FOUR DIFFERENT SURVEYS—OR MORE

Looking at history, the idea that you could survey or take a poll of vast numbers of people is a recent innovation. The first political opinion polls were taken during the 1824 presidential election between John Quincy Adams and Andrew Jackson. (Jackson won in the polls and popular vote, but Adams was made president by Congress.) In 1932, George Gallup, the father of modern polling, took his first public opinion survey in a local election in Iowa. In that same year, when Rensis Likert devised his innovative survey format, we had no computers and no digital databases. Results from a survey had to be recorded by hand, using a ledger or a manual typewriter. The scores had to be totaled using a mechanical adding machine. Even the advent of the punch card (old folks will remember the admonition "Do not fold, spindle, or mutilate") to record and store data didn't make the process any more agile.

Polling has always had a checkered past. One of the most notorious of botched political polls was the 1936 *Literary Digest* straw poll survey that concluded GOP presidential challenger Alf Landon would win in a landslide over the incumbent, Franklin Delano Roosevelt, with 57 percent of the vote. President Roosevelt won the 1936 election easily, with 63 percent of the vote, and the *Literary Digest* went bankrupt the following year.

In the digital age, we have access to vastly more powerful data collecting and analytical tools. But despite these technological advances, our approach to customer surveys is rooted in the twentieth century. We use "one-size-fits-all" surveys for every customer, regardless of their persona or expectations. We see a positive customer experience as following one "script." If our salespeople fail to adhere to the script, then we think they have displeased the customer.

In today's hyper-competitive marketplace, we must do much better. And with the digital tools available to us, we *can* do much better!

Think back to our discussion of the sales funnel, and how prospective customers are filtered as they move along toward a sale. Think also of the ubiquitous inbound phone tree system, where callers are routed to various destinations depending on their needs. When conducting a survey campaign, the same approach must be used. Instead of wasting time with meaningless demographic questions like the customer's age or gender, the survey subjects need to be sorted according to their *expectations*. Just a few questions will do it. For example, for a store called Smith's Supply, the first four survey questions could be this:

When I came to Smith's Supply, I wanted to:

A. Get in and out as quickly and efficiently as possible.

B.   Take time to get to know the store and its staff.

C.   Learn all I could about the product before I bought it.

D.   Have the opportunity to consult with my partner.

Because this is just a qualifying round, the respondent can be asked to choose the one that's closest to what they expected. This will ensure just one choice.

This is a form of "skip logic," which is a strategy that determines what set of questions the respondent is offered based on how they answered the current question. Also known as "conditional branching" or "branch logic," skip logic creates an individualized path through the survey that ensures the respondent sees questions that are relevant to their experience. Skip logic saves time for both you and your respondents, and reduces the likelihood that the respondent will become bored by questions that don't matter to them, or provide a random answer just to be done with it.

Survey for the Driver

Based on their choice, the respondent is then presented with one of four different surveys. The survey presented to Drivers will be different from the survey presented to Amiables, Analyticals, and Collaborators. The survey presented to Drivers will focus not only on the ubiquitous questions of product quality, but on questions designed to measure to what extent the company scored lovepoints and/or hatepoints based on the specific expectations of Drivers. Likewise for the other three personas; each will receive their own customized survey designed to measure how well the brand met their expectations.

After the initial qualifying question or questions, each respondent is presented with the survey appropriate for them. They are asked to answer two sets of questions. There should be no more than five in each set, for a maximum number of questions per set at ten, plus the initial qualifying question.

In the first set of five questions, the Driver respondent is asked about what she loved about the experience. In the second set of five questions, she's asked about what she disliked. We *want her* to tell us something she hated. The love-hate sequence goes like this:

> **Lovepoints.** Using the scale of 1 (unliked), 2 (liked), 3 (loved), or 4 (really loved), please indicate your level of *happiness* with the following five events:

> **A.** My interaction with the first salesperson I spoke to when I entered the store.

> **B.** My interaction with the salesperson who served me.

> **C.** How long I had to wait to pay.

> **D.** The availability of the exact product I wanted.

> **E.** The elapsed time it took for me to complete my purchase and leave the store.

> **Hatepoints.** Using the scale of 1 (not good), 2 (bad), 3 (hated), or 4 (really hated), please indicate your level of *dissatisfaction* with the following five events:

> **A.** How long I had to wait before a salesperson greeted me.

B. The time spent looking for the product I wanted.

C. The match between the actual product and what I had envisioned.

D. The checkout process.

E. The level of attentiveness of the salesperson to me and what I wanted.

As you can see, the questions presented in the two parts are similar but not exactly the same. The reason we ask specifically for what the customer may have hated was to give the customer "permission" to express her true feelings. We're asking her what she didn't like about her experience, and we want her to tell us.

Also note that these questions are particularly relevant to the values and expectations of a Driver. This customer knows what she wants to buy, and wants to get in and out as quickly as possible. She will have little concern for how "nice" the salesperson is, how well the product was explained, and even the appearance of the store.

There is one more very important caveat: because this person is a Driver, we should expect a low level of "love," with the possible exception of questions 1-D and 2-C, which relate to the product itself, which was the reason she came to the store. With a driver, your primary goal is to make the sales process smooth and painless. Drivers don't enjoy shopping for its own sake. They don't care if the auto dealer's service department has a snack bar or cable TV to watch in the customer lounge. They want to drop off their car, leave, and then come back to pick it up when it's ready. If you ask them about the comfort of the customer lounge, they'll become irritated because the question is irrelevant. With

Drivers, you want to eliminate hatepoints as much as possible, and then settle for a minimally positive set of lovepoints.

Survey for the Analytical

Now let's take a look at the same survey when presented to an Analytical. You will see that some of the questions are the same (functioning as a control set) while others are tailored for the Analytical's expectations:

> **Lovepoints.** Using the scale of 1 (unliked), 2 (liked), 3 (loved), or 4 (really loved), please tell us your level of *happiness* with the following five events:
>
> **A.** My interaction with the first salesperson I spoke to when I entered the store.
>
> **B.** My interaction with the salesperson who served me.
>
> **C.** The product information provided to me by the salesperson.
>
> **D.** My confidence in having chosen the product.
>
> **E.** The product return policy as explained to me.
>
> **Hatepoints.** Using the scale of 1 (not good), 2 (bad), 3 (hated), or 4 (really hated), please tell us your level of *dissatisfaction* with the following five events:
>
> **A.** My opportunity to look at all the possibilities without feeling rushed.

B. The time spent by the salesperson discussing the product I wanted.

C. The match between the actual product and what I had envisioned.

D. My confidence that the salesperson gave me the very best advice.

E. The level of attentiveness of the salesperson to me and what I wanted.

With an Analytic, you especially want to pay attention to the responses that relate to how well informed they feel, because this is likely to be the most important part of the experience for them.

Again, these are just hypothetical, sample questions. The questions you ask need to be tailored specifically for your business environment and customer base. A survey for an online business will be very different, as will a hotel's or a restaurant's. The point is that the RealRatings survey will provide you with highly specific, actionable information about what your customers love and hate *according to their individual expectations*. The slight redundancy of the love/hate questions will provide a verification of veracity (or not); for example, if a Driver expresses very low love for the time she had to wait to pay (question 1-C), you should expect her to express a correspondingly high level of hate for the checkout process (question 2-D).

In this book, I've presented four customer personas. This is just the most basic breakdown. In practice, your business could create as many customer personas as you believe to be necessary. If it were relevant, you could add demographic qualifiers like age, but only if you're certain that different age groups have different expectations—for instance, if they're shopping for different products. The trick, especially in phone surveys, is to quickly move them through the qualifying phase before they get bored and want to hang up. Online surveys will go more quickly because the respondent can read text much faster than an interviewer can recite the script.

Before the digital age, producing this level of agility and granularity would have been impossible. The data would have been too much to process, and the "phone tree" feature, where the respondent is instantly characterized according to his or her persona, didn't exist. Today, with our powerful databases and processing tools, it will be easy to construct a RealRatings survey system that presents to each respondent a survey that is concise and tailored precisely to their expectations.

The Question of "Leading" the Respondent

Traditional surveys are often faulted for including questions or statements that suggest how the respondent should answer. A leading question is one that pushes respondents to answer in a specific manner, based on the way the question is framed. Rather than trying to get a true and an unbiased answer to an issue question, such questions often contain embedded information that the survey creator wants to confirm.

For example, a leading question posited to a store customer might be, "How much did you enjoy your visit to Smith's Supply?" The answers might range from "not at all" to "very much." While subtle, the question is based on an assumption that the visit was pleasant, and steers the respondent toward a positive response, which would presumably please the store's managers.

A leading question may be based on an assumption plus a direct implication for the future: "If you enjoyed this conference, shall we offer another one next year?" Again, the respondent is subtly steered to answer "yes."

A dichotomous question is a question with only two possible answers—generally, "yes" or "no." Such a choice may be unbiased if it's used properly, but often you'll see it with questions that should have multiple choices, such as "I always buy organic food." The problem is that the words "always," "organic," and "food" are open to subjective interpretation, rendering the response worthless.

Some questions ask the respondent to imagine what other people might believe. For example, if you ask, "Should concerned parents use infant car seats?" you're not asking the respondent for his or her personal opinion, but their opinion of what people in general should believe. The response will not be a precisely accurate reflection of the intentions of the respondent.

"Double-barreled" questions mash two questions together that should be separate. For example, let's say a restaurant asks, "Do you always have coffee and dessert after dinner?" This question has multiple problems! The first is the use of the word "always," which we know is inappropriate. The second is the combining of "coffee" and "dessert," because you can have one without the other. They need to be separate questions, such as, "The last time you ate in a restaurant, after dinner did you order coffee? Did you order a dessert?"

Surveys are too often written by people with either a conscious or unconscious bias toward eliciting a favorable—or at least not unfavorable—response from the consumer toward the brand. This is all part of the psychology of wanting to know what people love, and then looking for evidence that, yes, in some way my customer loves my brand, service, or product. And then, how can we give them more of what they love?

There is logic to this. Every business wants to give people what they love. The powerful message behind the RealRatings system is that we also must find out what our customers *hate*, and then take action to reduce it. To the question of whether the RealRatings questions have an implicit bias, the answer is "yes." Each set of questions—lovepoints and hatepoints—is based on the real-world fact that in every customer's journey across all the touchpoints, there will be times when the customer loves the experience, and times when he or she hates it. Remember, it's physically impossible for any organization to deliver a 100 percent perfect experience. It's impossible to provide a service that's equally fast, low-cost, high quality, and ethical. You cannot have all four at one time. You must sacrifice one of them.

So we are up front in asking the customer, what parts of the experience did you love? The questions are openly designed to steer the customer toward what they loved about their experience. Then, we're equally up front about asking the customer what they disliked. There's no pretense. We want to know where we failed!

Scoring

There are two ways to score the results.

- **Overall score.** Here you simply add up all the lovepoints and hatepoints, and then subtract one from the other. The result is a score that tells you your customer's overall opinion based on the touchpoints included in the survey.

  In the RealRatings system, the respondent is asked to provide an answer to every question. Therefore, in a survey with five questions, the total number of lovepoints could range from a low of 5 to a high of 20. The same applies to the hatepoints.

  To get the overall score, you subtract the hatepoints from the lovepoints.

The maximum love shown by your customer to your brand could be 20 lovepoints minus 5 hatepoints = 15 points. This is as good as it gets.

The maximum hate shown by your customer to your brand could be 5 lovepoints minus 20 hatepoints = negative 15. This is as bad as it gets.

In this book I've argued that surveys with one score are blunt instruments and not very useful. This is true. The overall RealRating score gives you a general picture of how your customers perceive you, and is useful as a comparison for year-over-year, assuming you use the same survey.

- **Item scores.** The true power of the RealRating system lies in its ability to pinpoint areas of love and hate, and then allow you to drill down with greater specificity. Let's say you ask a group of customers ten questions, and the results show a high level of hate and a corresponding shortfall of love for their experience on your website. Websites are complicated things, and this alone doesn't tell you much. Based on this insight, you need to do two things:

  1. Analyze your visitor data from your website. Find out the number of visitors, which pages they linger on, how long they stay, how many abandon their shopping carts—all the usual metrics that a website generates.

  2. Write another survey that specifically asks about the website experience. Now, instead of just one question about the website, you can have a series, each targeting a different aspect. Tabulate the results. See which aspect stands out. Perhaps the navigation produces the most hate, and prospects are giving up the search for what they want. You can fix the problem and then sur-

vey your customers again. It's an efficient and cost-effective approach!

BRINGING IT ALL TOGETHER

The RealRatings system is a multidimensional approach that provides far better insights than traditional surveys. Additionally, since customer experience is an innovation activity, it provides you with the design inputs you need to architect and design the best possible human experiences.

When we develop surveys for our clients, we are very careful about the linguistics of the questions to make certain that we factor in the likely perception of the question across a range of personas. The survey industry has made a fortune by turning the thoughtful process of understanding our customers into a "black box" that they make a fortune on. To do this right requires a more surgical application of these principles.

I've been tricked by the customer experience industrial complex myself. There is definitely a warm, comfortable feeling in pushing out a survey. It's easy, low risk, and it produces beautiful charts and graphs. However, leveraging a multidimensional approach that gleans insights across the hate/love spectrum is far better. This will give you the insights to deliver exceptional experiences across all touchpoints and throughout a range of customer personas. It's worth it! There's absolutely no question that the best way to rapidly and positively impact your customer experience is to understand in great detail what they hate and what they love. Collecting and analyzing hatepoints provides the opportunity to quickly correct the negative experiences that could be killing your enterprise.

Customer Experience Innovation Strategy

If you want to develop customer impact, stakeholder adoption, and measurable returns on investment, then you must have a formal customer experience strategy. Your plan should have subordinate plans that support the tactical implementation to include:

- Detailed customer experience innovation goals and expected outcomes.

- Connection to the overarching mission of the organization.

- Cross-departmental team architecture.

- Internal communication plan that leverages a collaboration resource.

- If possible, a formal strategy for a center for customer experience innovation.

- Thoughtful KPIs that are not based just on financial returns. These should include return on mission, brand, and long-term customer satisfaction impact.

- Graphic reporting instruments that include executive dashboards.

- Thoughtful and significantly improved means of gaining authentic customer insights, led by the use of the RealRatings survey system.

- Other tactical deployments required based on your organization and industry.

TAKE ACTION!

Using the four main customer personas—Driver, Analytical, Amiable, and Collaborator—as a starting point, and thanks to advances in digital data collection and management, we can survey customers based on *their individual expectations* of what they want from their touchpoint journey. This approach is based on the idea that what one customer loves, another customer might hate, and the touchpoint journey must be adaptable to each persona.

Then, using the RealRatings system, we can learn from our customers exactly what they love about the company, brand, or service, and what they hate. Both responses are equally necessary and useful. Our goal is to increase the lovepoints while decreasing the hatepoints.

This is all part of the overall customer experience strategy (CXS), which must be a core part of the organization's everyday operations as well as its long-term plan for growth and success. An unrelenting focus on reducing what customers hate about your business will lead to happier lifelong customers, easier and more frequent sales, higher revenues, and a brighter future in a very competitive world.

THANK YOU FOR READING

Thank you for reading *What Customers Hate*. The intention of this book is to challenge the framework and beliefs of the traditional customer experience "best practice." Getting out of your comfort zone and taking a fresh look at the problem requires courage and a willingness to be open to new ideas. The principles revealed on these pages are based on a lifetime of study and have been used in my own practice with significant success across multiple industries and organizations. I trust that your application of these practical solutions will serve you and your organization well.

My most sincere thanks—and I wish you every success!

NOTES

CHAPTER 1

1. *Car and Driver*. https://www.caranddriver.com/news/a34992832/battery -price-drop-2023/.

2. Brex.com. https://www.brex.com/blog/what-is-a-good-profit-margin /#:~:text=An%20NYU%20report%20on%20U.S.,20%25%20is%20a%20 high%20margin.

3. *TIME*. https://time.com/5629233/amazon-warehouse-employee-treatment -robots/.

4. DigitalCommerce360. https://www.digitalcommerce360.com/article /amazon-sales/#:~:text=quarter%2C%20ending%20Dec.-,31%2C%20 2020%2C%20Amazon%20reported%3A,the%20prior%20year's%20 %2436.90%20billion.

CHAPTER 2

1. *Business Insider*. https://www.businessinsider.com/uber-lyft-having -devastating-effect-on-public-transportation-study-2019-1.

2. Recruiterbox. https://recruiterbox.com/blog/how-negative-employee -reviews-hurt-employer-brand-and-how-to-stop-them.

CHAPTER 4

1. https://www.mediapost.com/publications/article/201157/shoppers -prefer-personalized-brick-mortar-vs-on.html?print#axzz2VYmFamie.

2. Cornell Law School. https://www.law.cornell.edu/wex/bait_and_switch #:~:text=A%20E2%80%9Cbait%20and%20switch%E2%80%9D%20

takes,not%20actually%20intend%20to%20sell.&text=A%20%E2%80%9
Cbait%20and%20switch%E2%80%9D%20is%20also%20a%20violation
%20of%20the,and%20Deceptive%20Business%20Practices%20Act.

3. HBS. https://digital.hbs.edu/platform-digit/submission/23andme-losing
-at-digital-privacy/.

CHAPTER 5

1. Nielsen. https://www.nielsen.com/us/en/insights/report/2012/global
-trust-in-advertising-and-brand-messages-2/.

2. Influencer Marketing Hub. https://influencermarketinghub.com
/influencer-marketing-benchmark-report-2021/.

3. *Entrepreneur.* https://www.entrepreneur.com/article/285613#:~:text=
According%20to%20recent%20reports%2C%20social,often%20than
%20any%20other%20leads.

4. *TIME.* http://content.time.com/time/specials/2007/0,28757,1658545,00
.html.

5. *Philadelphia Inquirer.* https://www.inquirer.com/philly/business/20140930
_Comcast_names_a_top_exec_to_fix_bad_customer_service.html.

6. ABC News. https://abcnews.go.com/Business/comcast-apologizes
-unacceptable-customer-service-call-end/story?id=24567047.

7. Elliott.org. https://www.elliott.org/is-this-enough-compensation/comcast
-thinks-husband-ahole-put-writing/.

8. *Forbes.* https://www.forbes.com/sites/micahsolomon/2017/11/06/turning
-the-customer-ship-around-how-comcast-yes-comcast-has-been-working
-to-improve/?sh=365688a7753b.

9. Fiercetelecom. https://www.fiercetelecom.com/telecom/how-comcast
-changed-customer-care-landscape-its-digital-tools-during-covid-19.

10. CXOTalk. https://www.cxotalk.com/episode/customer-experience
-transformation-comcast.

11. CXOTalk. https://www.cxotalk.com/episode/customer-experience
-transformation-comcast.

12. Bizjournals.com. https://www.bizjournals.com/philadelphia/news/2020
/06/09/comcast-customer-satisfaction-acsi-survey.html.

CHAPTER 6

1. https://www.amazon.com/Golden-Opportunity-Remarkable-Careers -McDonalds/dp/1604332794/ref=sr_1_1?dchild=1&keywords=%E2%80 %9CGolden+Opportunity%3A+Remarkable+Careers+That+Began+at +McDonald%E2%80%99s.%E2%80%9D&qid=1618850227&sr=8-1.

CHAPTER 7

1. QuoteInvestigator. https://quoteinvestigator.com/2011/07/28/ford-faster -horse/.

2. Ibid.

3. *Isaacson.* https://www.amazon.com/Steve-Jobs-Walter-Isaacson/dp /1451648537.

4. Apple. https://jobs.apple.com/en-us/details/200233451/iphone-market -research-analysis-manager.

5. Apple. https://jobs.apple.com/en-us/details/200233451/iphone-market -research-analysis-manager?team=MKTG.

6. *Wall Street Journal.* https://www.wsj.com/articles/BL-DGB-24752.

CHAPTER 8

1. Vox.com. https://www.vox.com/2014/4/25/5647696/the-way-we-board -airplanes-makes-absolutely-no-sense.

2. Statista. https://www.statista.com/statistics/539278/customer-complaints -by-us-airlines/#:~:text=U.S.%20airlines%20by%20rate%20of%20customer %20complaints%202020&text=This%20statistic%20represents%20the %20U.S.,enplanements%20on%20domestic%2Dscheduled%20operations.

3. *Fast Company.* https://www.fastcompany.com/3052604/how-ikea-designs -its-infamous-instruction-manuals.

4. *New York Times.* https://www.nytimes.com/2017/09/28/business /ikea-taskrabbit.html?mcubz=0&_r=0.

5. *Business Insider.* https://www.businessinsider.com/ikea-help-assemble -furniture-taskrabbit-2018-1.

6. NBC News. https://www.nbcnews.com/id/wbna37238500.

7. Teen Ink. https://www.teenink.com/hot_topics/what_matters/article/342939/Why-I-Hate-Facebook.

8. *New Yorker*. https://www.newyorker.com/magazine/2020/10/19/why-facebook-cant-fix-itself.

9. Mashable. https://mashable.com/article/why-we-dont-delete-facebook-account/.

CHAPTER 9

1. Pegasystems. https://www.pega.com/system/files/resources/2019-09/the-good-the-bad-the-ugly.pdf.

2. Walt Disney Co. https://www.disneyinstitute.com/blog/customer-service-101-happiness-is-a-purple-balloon/.

CHAPTER 10

1. Medium. https://medium.com/the-mission/employee-performance-depends-on-these-3-critical-factors-4393b5b2f90e.

CHAPTER 11

1. Nielsen. https://nielseniq.com/global/en/insights/report/2015/looking-to-achieve-new-product-success/.

2. Federal Reserve. https://fred.stlouisfed.org/series/OPHNFB.

3. TCM.net. http://www.tmcnet.com/articles/comsol/0100/0100pubout.htm.

4. BankMyCell.com. https://www.bankmycell.com/support/e-waste-cell-phone-recycling-facts#stats1.

5. *Business Insider*. https://www.businessinsider.com/how-airbnb-was-founded-a-visual-history-2016-2#in-september-2019-airbnb-announced-its-plan-to-go-public-in-2020-29.

CHAPTER 12

1. SHRM. https://www.shrm.org/about-shrm/press-room/press-releases /pages/shrm-reports-toxic-workplace-cultures-cost-billions.aspx#:~:text =NEW%20YORK%20%E2%80%94%20One%20in%20five,SHRM%20 report%20on%20workplace%20culture.

2. *Harvard Business Review.* https://hbr.org/2018/03/the-economics -of-why-companies-dont-fix-their-toxic-cultures.

3. EBN. https://www.benefitnews.com/news/employee-stress-lost -productivity-costing-employers-billions.

4. Officevibe. https://officevibe.com/blog/employee-surveys-infographic.

5. https://www.linkedin.com/pulse/stop-wasting-money-benefits-employees -dont-value-nishal-mistri/.

6. https://www.comparably.com/news/happiest-employees-2020/.

7. Zoom. https://zoom.us/.

CHAPTER 13

1. Retaildive. https://www.retaildive.com/spons/whats-wrong-with-retailers -customer-surveys/525124/.

2. PewResearch. https://www.pewresearch.org/fact-tank/2019/02/27 /response-rates-in-telephone-surveys-have-resumed-their-decline/.

3. Quirks.com. https://www.quirks.com/articles/why conventional-customer -surveys-create-a-false-sense-of-security.

CHAPTER 14

1. SurveyAnyPlace.com. https://surveyanyplace.com/survey-fatigue/.

2. mTab. http://www.mtab.com/why-people-lie-on-customer-surveys-and -how-to-minimize-it/.

INDEX

CONTACT THE AUTHOR

Nick is always excited to learn about how his readers have applied his methods to drive world-class customer experience in their own organizations. He can be contacted through his consulting and training firm at www.mylearnlogic.com or for speaking engagements at www.nickwebb.com.

ABOUT THE AUTHOR

Nick Webb is one of the top customer experience and customer service experts in the world. He has been awarded the Global Gurus Top 30 designation for customer service for seven years in a row. Nick is the CEO of goLeaderLogic.com, a customer experience training and advisory firm that works with some of the top brands to help them build world-class customer experiences.

As a technologist, he has been awarded more than forty US patents for consumer and technology products.

Nick is the author of multiple number one bestselling books in the areas of business innovation, customer experience, and leadership. He is also one of the top keynote speakers in the areas of business growth, innovation, future trends, and customer experience.